INSTITUTE OF LEADERSHIP & MANAGEMENT ilm

SUPERSERIES

Achieving
Quality

FOURTH EDITION

Published for the
Institute of Leadership & Management by **Pergamon Flexible Learning**

OXFORD   AMSTERDAM   BOSTON   LONDON   NEW YORK   PARIS
SAN DIEGO   SAN FRANCISCO   SINGAPORE   SYDNEY   TOKYO

Pergamon Flexible Learning
An imprint of Elsevier
Linacre House, Jordan Hill, Oxford OX2 8DP
200 Wheeler Road, Burlington, MA 01803

First published 1986
Second edition 1991
Third edition 1997
Fourth edition 2003
Reprinted 2004

British Library Cataloguing in Publication Data
A catalogue record for this book is available from the British Library

ISBN 0 7506 5874 6

For information on Pergamon Flexible Learning
visit our website at www.bh.com/pergamonfl

Institute of Leadership & Management
registered office
1 Giltspur Street
London
EC1A 9DD
Telephone 020 7294 3053
www.i-l-m.com
ILM is part of the City & Guilds Group

The views expressed in this work are those of the authors and do
not necessarily reflect those of the Institute of Leadership &
Management or of the publisher.

Authors: Bob Foley and Joe Johnson
Editor: Heather Serjeant
Editorial management: Genesys, www.genesys-consultants.com
Based on previous material by Joe Johnson
Composition by Genesis Typesetting Limited, Rochester, Kent
Printed and bound in Great Britain by MPG Books, Bodmin

Contents

Contents

Workbook introduction

1 ILM Super Series study links

This workbook addresses the issues of *Achieving Quality*. Should you wish to extend your study to other Super Series workbooks covering related or different subject areas, you will find a comprehensive list at the back of this book.

2 Links to ILM qualifications

This workbook relates to the following learning outcomes in segments from the ILM Level 3 Introductory Certificate in First Line Management and the Level 3 Certificate in First Line Management.

C5.5   Delivering Quality
1   Explain the meaning and purpose of quality
2   Contribute to the management of quality
3   Identify relevant aspects of ISO 9000:2000
4   Apply simple systems for quality control
5   Identify and use statistical methods as appropriate to the organization

C5.8   Statistical Process Control
1   Understand the concept and benefits of statistical process control
2   Construct and interpret control charts for variable and attribute data
3   Take appropriate action in response to charts

3 Links to S/NVQs in Management

This workbook relates to the following elements of the Management Standards which are used in S/NVQs in Management, as well as a range of other S/NVQs.

A1.1   Maintain work activities to meet requirements

A1.3   Make recommendations for improvements to work activities

It is designed to help you demonstrate the following Personal Competences:

- building teams;
- communicating;
- focusing on results;
- thinking and taking decisions.

4 Workbook objectives

In a more competitive world organizations will only survive if they can guarantee quality in their goods or their services. Short-term profit at the expense of quality will lead to short-term lives. In that sense quality is, to my mind, the organizational equivalent of truth. Quality like truth will count, in the end. No one, and no organization, can live a lie for long.[1]

Does your organization try to cover up the truth? Does it pay lip-service to quality? Or do you believe it has quality so firmly in its sights that it has nothing to hide?

This workbook is about quality in organizations. You should find it interesting: it encompasses a broad spectrum of ideas and aspects of the subject.

[1] Charles Handy, *The Age of Unreason*, p. 115. Arrow Books Ltd.

There are four sessions. Session A is intended to be a general discussion of quality: what it is, what it's for, and how it can be achieved. Having set the scene, in Session B we home in on standards, and specifically ISO 9000:2000, the quality systems standard. We'll look in some detail at what this standard contains.

Sessions C and D are rather more technical: they deal with statistics, and statistical process control (SPC). We will attempt to answer the question: 'Having set up your work process to achieve a defined level of quality, how can you keep it under control?'

4.1 Objectives

When you have completed this workbook you will be better able to:

- explain the meaning and purpose of quality;
- describe some sound approaches to quality management;
- summarize the contents and purpose of ISO 9000:2000;
- carry out simple statistical calculations related to quality control;
- recognize how the techniques of statistical process control can be usefully applied to work processes.

5 Activity planner

You may want to look at the following Activities now, so that you can start collecting material as soon as possible.

Activity 4 on page 10 where you are asked to recommend a way to improve your team's performance.

Activity 6 on page 19 which asks you to describe your own team's work as a system in terms of inputs, processes and outputs.

Activity 20 on page 51 where you are asked to consider how your own job's processes should be monitored and measured, and then to devise and carry out an audit program on one or two processes.

Some or all of these Activities may provide the basis of evidence for your S/NVQ portfolio. All Portfolio Activities and the Work-based assignment are signposted with this icon.

The icon states the elements to which the Portfolio Activities and Work-based assignment relate.

In the Work-based assignment on page 104 you are given the choice of (a) finding ways to apply statistical process control to your team's work or (b) selecting an area of quality management, and drawing up a brief report which explains how your team can contribute more effectively to the organization's quality system or procedures. Both these tasks are designed to help you meet elements A1.1 and A1.3; they will also contribute to elements D1.1 and D1.2 of the Management Standards: 'Gather required information', and 'Inform and advise others'. You may want to prepare for the assignment in advance.

Session A
Quality in context

1 Introduction

> The heart of quality is not a technique. It is a commitment by management to its people and product – stretching over a period of decades and lived with persistence and passion – that is unknown in most organizations today.[1]

The book by Peters and Austin was first published in 1985. There's been a growing interest in quality management since that time, but if the criticism implied in the second sentence was valid then, the situation won't have changed very much – there hasn't been time. If you are lucky, you may have noticed a maturing commitment to quality among senior management in your organization. At any rate, you will perhaps be aware of the increased importance given generally to the management of quality.

The last two sessions of this workbook are about techniques: statistics, sampling and quality control. However, as Peters and Austin say, techniques are not at the heart of quality. It is important, therefore, to begin by discussing some more fundamental issues, before we get on to numbers and statistics.

We start by defining what we mean by quality. Then we discuss the management aspects, and the steps involved in achieving high quality.

We'll round off the session by briefly investigating the subject of Total Quality Management, and achieving quality at team level.

The Super Series workbook *Understanding Quality* would be a good place to start if you want to learn more about the subject of quality in general.

---

[1] Tom Peters and Nancy Austin, writing in *A Passion for Excellence*, p. 101. First published in the USA by Random House (1985). First published in Great Britain by William Collins: Fontana/Collins (1985).

2 The meaning of quality

When you want to buy something – a radio, say, or a haircut – there's usually a choice of suppliers, and brands or styles. So even if you have a very clear idea of what you're looking for, a decision has to be made.

2.1 The starting point for quality

It is the decisions made by customers like you that determine the quality of goods and services.

Activity 1

4 mins

Suppose you intend to purchase a fairly expensive item of household equipment – say a washing machine or vacuum cleaner.

What would influence the choice you make? Jot down **four** factors that would influence your choice.

_____

_____

_____

_____

There may be a number of factors influencing your decision, including perhaps:

- your experience when using similar products in the past;
- the price: how much you are prepared to pay, and how one model compares in price with another;

- the features available on each model;
- a recommendation of a particular product by a friend;
- what machines a shop has in stock;
- the colour and appearance of the product;
- whether the manufacturer has a reputation for the reliability of its products;
- delivery (can you have the product when you need it?);
- the persuasiveness of the shop salesperson;
- whether the goods meet agreed safety standards;
- the size of the product (will the machine fit in your kitchen?).

All these factors have some bearing on the quality of the goods. Your final choice of product will differ from that of many other people because you have different needs from them. Producers and suppliers have to take careful note of the choices made by potential customers. If they try to market a product that people don't want, they are bound to fail.

The starting point for quality is in the wants and needs of customers.

2.2 The definition of quality

What exactly do we mean by the word quality?

Here is the 'official' definition, given in the International Organization for Standardization's ISO 9000:2000 *Quality Management Systems: Fundamentals and Vocabulary*.

Quality is the: 'degree to which a set of characteristics fulfils requirements'.

This has been restated in a number of ways. One way to summarize it is to say that:

Quality is fitness for purpose.

Activity 2 · 3 mins

A book is published first in hardback form, with superior binding and on expensive paper. Later the same book is published as a paperback, on cheap paper.

Which book, if any, is of the higher quality? Give a brief reason for your answer.

_____

_____

_____

You may have said that the hardback book was of higher quality. This would be a common understanding of the word 'quality'. A hardback book feels and looks better, and an advertisement describing the hardback book might talk about 'quality paper' or 'quality materials'.

But we have said that quality is fitness for purpose. If a product becomes too expensive for the customers it is aimed at, because inappropriate materials are used, it won't sell. The hardback book will suit certain customers, but many others would sooner wait for the paperback. Both products are designed with the needs of their intended customers in mind. Neither is inherently of higher quality than the other.

A producer (such as a bicycle manufacturer, or a book publisher) generates goods or services for sale. A supplier (such as a flower shop, or an insurance agent) offers goods or services for sale.

So every producer and supplier has to make a decision as to the quality required by customers. If the quality of a product is not appropriate for their needs and wants – using materials that are too expensive, perhaps, or too cheap – people will not buy it (or will not continue to buy it).

3 Ensuring quality

If quality is determined by the needs, wants or expectations of customers, or potential customers, how can a producer or supplier go about meeting those needs?

The process can be expressed in terms of four steps: four questions that the organization must answer:

1 What do customers need or want?

2 Are our products meeting those wants?

3 How can we specify new or modified products to meet those wants?

4 How can we make sure that our products match, and continue to match, our own specifications?

From now on, we'll use the word 'product' to include any kind of goods or services. This definition is supported by ISO 9000, as we will discuss later.

The first two steps are in the domain of marketing, and the questions can be answered by conducting activities such as:

- carrying out market research;
- talking to customers and potential customers;
- studying competitors' products;
- analysing product performance;
- investigating technological developments;
- keeping abreast of fashion trends.

Answering the third and fourth questions requires an understanding of **design quality** and **process quality**. These terms are defined as follows.

Design quality: the degree to which the specification of the product satisfies customers' wants and expectations. (Is it the right product?)

Process quality, or the quality of conformance: the degree to which the product conforms to specifications, when it is transferred to the customer. (Are we producing it right?)

In Session B we will discuss design quality. In Sessions C and D, our focus will be on process quality. We will look at some statistical techniques that are used in controlling the quality of goods and services

3.1 Being precise about quality

However, it is important to remember that you can control quality only after you have defined the standards you want to reach. It's not enough to talk in vague generalities, encouraging employees to 'use high quality materials', or 'work to the very best of your abilities'. Getting quality right means being very specific and detailed about how you want your product to perform: how you intend to meet your customers' needs.

Any reputable manufacturer will go to great lengths to specify dimensions, materials, construction methods, test methods, performance criteria and so on.

A service provider may find it more difficult to be so explicit about the standards of quality expected. It takes more thought if you want to give detailed instructions to sales staff about the level of friendliness required, or give precise guidelines to nurses regarding the amount of attention they should give to patients in particular circumstances. Although these are difficult questions, they must be addressed.

What we mean by quality in any complex organization is likely to be determined by a whole range of judgements. Many organizations are continuing to put a lot of effort into setting standards that are not easily measured in terms of output or defect rates.

3.2 Getting the quality right

Who is responsible for the quality of the product or service with which you are associated?

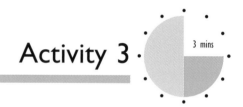

Activity 3

3 mins

Which people in your current (or a previous) organization are responsible for ensuring the quality of its products?

The teams of people who do the work	☐
The people who check the work	☐
First line managers	☐
Top management	☐
All of the above	☐

The answer can be found on page 117.

The quality of a company's products and services is a reflection of the organization of that company and of the training and attitudes of its management and employees.

Getting the quality right means:

■ **A clear commitment from higher management**

If management are not interested in quality, then they should not be surprised if the company gets a reputation for poor quality.

■ **The setting of well-defined standards**

Everyone needs to know what he or she is aiming at. If standards are unclear, there is bound to be great variability.

■ **Providing the resources that will enable those standards to be reached**

The word 'resources' includes: people, workspace, materials, equipment, finance and training.

■ **Allowing and encouraging employees to be responsible for the quality of their own work**

Getting the quality right means not only setting standards, but giving people the opportunity to take full responsibility for meeting those standards.

The old idea of making those in the production department responsible for production targets, and making the quality control department responsible for quality targets, has been shown not to work.

■ **Setting a culture for quality**

It is a fact of life that most people tend to set their standards by the behaviour of those around them. If management behave as if they care about quality, the rest of the staff will be much more inclined to follow suit.

EXTENSION I
For practical advice on improving quality, see H. J. Harrington's *Business Process Improvement*

■ **Being consistent**

Not all suppliers are clear what quality standards they expect their products to reach.

Tanya Shipley went into a high street store on Wednesday, and was served by a courteous, helpful and well-informed assistant. Feeling happy about the service she got, Tanya returned to the same store on Saturday, to make another purchase. This time, once she managed to get the attention of a member of staff, she found him to be surly, lacking in knowledge about the product, and off-hand in answering her questions. When she complained, Tanya got an apology from the manager, who said: 'Oh, he is temporary Saturday staff – what can you expect?'

Consistency is a key
aspect of quality.

What Tanya expected was a consistently high level of service. As a customer, she was not very interested in the problems the store had in achieving this standard of quality.

■ Ensuring that quality standards are consistently adhered to

This is what is usually meant by **quality assurance** and **quality control**.

3.3 Quality assurance and quality control

The definition of **quality assurance** is

> Part of quality management focused on providing confidence that quality requirements will be fulfilled (ISO 9000:2000)

Quality control is part of quality assurance. It consists of the operational techniques and activities that are used to fulfil requirements for quality, and which are the focus of the last two sessions of this workbook.

Let's repeat the main points of this section.

■ Producers and suppliers need to know their customers' wants, and whether their products are meeting those wants.
■ They must then specify the goods and services they intend to produce or supply: that's **design quality**.
■ The next stage is to ensure that the defined quality standards are adhered to: that's **process quality**, and it's achieved through systems of **quality assurance** and **quality control**.
■ Quality is the responsibility of **everyone** in the organization.
■ Achieving quality depends on management:

  ■ displaying commitment;
  ■ setting standards;
  ■ providing resources;
  ■ allowing employees to take responsibility for standards;
  ■ setting a culture for quality.

4 Total quality management

In the long term, organizations compete on the basis of their product or service quality; TQM is therefore seen as an approach to gaining or sustaining a competitive lead.[2]

Achieving quality, including getting accreditation to ISO 9000:2000 or other standards, is no easy journey to make.

Experience shows that a piecemeal approach is ineffective. Organizations that tackle quality problems in isolation, or work on the assumption that quality is some magical ingredient to be sprinkled on to taste, generally come to grief.

Quality is not separate from the product: it is an integral part of the whole and all its parts. It follows that you cannot 'add on quality'; neither can you 'inspect in quality'. Quality must be:

- built in through every stage;
- intrinsic to every process;
- an essential element within every component.

The implication, therefore, is that quality must be total, and must involve every person and every activity. The term generally used for this 'holistic' approach is **Total Quality Management (TQM)**.

We can define TQM as follows.

Total Quality Management involves every member of the organization in a process of continuous improvement with the aim of satisfying the customers' wants and expectations.

The aims of quality, as we have already agreed, are to satisfy the customer. What about continuous improvement?

4.1 Continuous improvement

Continuous improvement is often referred to by its Japanese name, **kaizen**. It means carrying out many (perhaps small) detailed improvements to products, procedures and practices, over a long period.

Teams and individuals are expected to search for better ways of doing things, and for higher standards.

[2] Dennis F. Kehoe in *The Fundamentals of Quality Management*, p. 89. Chapman and Hall. First edition (1996).

Some examples of the way things might be improved are:

- putting by-products to good use, instead of throwing them away;
- analysing the order in which the steps of a process should be carried out, so as to find the most efficient and effective sequence;
- finding better ways to communicate detailed instructions to individuals;
- reorganizing a team, so that each member gets the chance to make better use of his or her skills and knowledge;
- encouraging people to talk more about mutual problems;
- setting aside prejudices;
- eliminating unnecessary bureaucracy;
- identifying ways of making the job more interesting and less of a drudge.

Activity 4

15 mins

 S/NVQ A1.3

This Activity is the first of a series of three which together may provide the basis of appropriate evidence for your S/NVQ portfolio. The others are Activities 6 and 20. If you are intending to take this course of action, it might be better to write your answers on separate sheets of paper.

Your aim in this Activity is to recommend a way to improve your team's performance.

Remember that, as a manager, you are most effective when you are able to give your team members the opportunity to make their own improvements. So one recommendation or action by you should, ideally, trigger off a whole series of improvements.

You may want to spend some time thinking about your team's work: their workspace; the pressures on individuals; their efficiency; their performance in comparison with other teams; their morale; their powers to take the initiative.

When you have identified a specific means of effecting improvement, write it down in detail on a separate sheet of paper.

5 Achieving quality at team level

If you are a first line manager working for a producer or supplier, you have a responsibility for the work done by your team, and for the quality of the goods and services you provide.

Activity 5

10 mins

How do you ensure that the required levels of quality are met? Tick whichever of the following you consider to be important in achieving quality in your job, and then say how each action is implemented in practice.

What do you do?		How do you do it?
■ I let the team know the standards of quality expected by me and the organization.	☐	
■ I demonstrate that I am just as concerned about quality as meeting other team goals, or controlling costs.	☐	
■ I take complete responsibility for the quality of my team's work	☐	
■ I take steps to ensure that training and other resources are provided, so that my team members are able to perform effectively.	☐	
■ I encourage the team in their efforts to raise standards.	☐	
■ I check the team's work while it is in progress.	☐	
■ I check the quality of the completed work (perhaps by sampling a percentage of the output).	☐	
■ I check just about everything that every team member does.	☐	

Let's discuss each of these points.

■ **Letting the team know the standards of quality you and the organization expect**

This is certainly important, as we've already mentioned. Even when quality standards have already been set by others – designers, managers or other departments – the first line manager retains responsibility for:

■ making sure the standards are understood;
■ imposing higher standards than the minimum, wherever possible;
■ leading the way by personal example.

A crucial part of your role is to help get the quality message across.

■ **Demonstrating a concern for quality**

Although this point seems similar to the last, there's a world of difference between simply passing on information about quality, and taking an active role in promoting quality. In your team meetings, how often is quality mentioned? And what kinds of decisions do you make when there's a conflict between:

■ costs and quality ('The price of this material has gone up. Can we get away with using something cheaper?');
■ output and quality ('We've got customers waiting – if we check it again, we may lose them.').

Your attitude to quality will be noticed and copied by your team.

■ **Taking complete responsibility for the quality of the team's work**

Your response to this one may have been: 'It depends what you mean'. Certainly the team leader takes responsibility for the team, but that doesn't mean to say that he or she carries the whole burden. As already discussed, quality is everybody's responsibility.

■ **Taking steps to provide training and other resources**

Yes, most would agree that this is part of the team leader's job. Above all, the leader is a facilitator – someone who removes obstacles, and empowers the team to achieve its goals.

■ **Encouraging the team to raise standards**

This is part of setting the right climate for quality. Sometimes remarkable progress can be made, simply by making the occasional supportive remark, especially at times when other pressures might make it easier to let standards fall.

The way you answered the last three points:

- checking work while in progress;
- checking completed work;
- checking just about everything;

will depend on your own team and job. Too much interference can be stifling and discouraging. Too little monitoring may allow standards to fall. Getting the balance right is part of the challenge of management.

So far in this workbook the word 'standards' has already appeared many times. But we need to be more specific about what it means. Standards are the subject of the next session.

Self-assessment 1

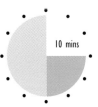

10 mins

1 Explain what is wrong with the following statements.

a Quality is another word for 'superior'.

_____

_____

_____

b The organization's quality experts have the main responsibility for quality.

_____

_____

c The marketing and design of a product is quite separate from its quality aspects.

_____

_____

d Quality is everyone's business, so managers have no special role to play.

_____

_____

2 Match each definition on the left with the correct term, taken from the list on the right. Some may be used more than once.

a Fitness for purpose.

b The totality of features and characteristics of a product or service that bear on its ability to satisfy stated or implied needs.

c The degree to which the specification of the product satisfies customers' wants and expectations.

d The degree to which the product conforms to specifications, when it is transferred to the customer.

e The operational techniques and activities that are used to fulfil requirements for quality.

i Process quality

ii Quality control

iii Quality

iv Conformance quality

v Design quality

Answers to these questions can be found on page 113.

6 Summary

■ The **needs of customers** is the starting point for quality.

■ Quality can be summarized as **fitness for purpose**.

■ Producers and suppliers need to know their customers' wants, and whether their **products are meeting those wants**.

■ They must then specify the goods and services they intend to produce or supply: that's **design quality**.

■ The next stage is to ensure the defined quality standards are adhered to: that's **process (or conformance) quality**, and it's achieved through systems of quality assurance and quality control.

■ Quality is the responsibility of **everyone** in the organization.

■ **Achieving quality** depends on management:

  ■ displaying commitment;
  ■ setting standards;
  ■ providing resources;
  ■ allowing employees to take responsibility for standards;
  ■ setting a culture for quality.

■ **Total Quality Management (TQM)** involves every member of the organization in a process of **continuous improvement** with the aim of satisfying the customers' wants and expectations.

Session B
Standards

1 Introduction

In Session A we said that getting the quality right means (among other things) setting well-defined standards. But who sets the standards used by your organization?

Many will be set internally. After all, you want your company's product to be higher quality than anybody else's. But it is also often useful – and sometimes essential – to have general standards, set by independent bodies, that are adhered to by your company and all your competitors.

Consequently there are a number of independent national and international bodies that publish formal standards on all manner of subjects.

In the UK the British Standards Institution (BSI) is the primary standards-setting body. There is also a European body called the Comité Européen de Normalisation (CEN) and an international body called the International Organization for Standardization (ISO).

- British Standards use the identifier 'BS'
- European Standards are identified with 'EN'
- International Standards are identified with 'ISO'
- Standards produced by CEN and/or ISO that have been **adopted** as British Standards are identified with the appropriate combination of letters, for example, 'BS EN ISO'.

Our main concern in this chapter is **quality systems standards**, and most of this chapter is devoted to the **BS EN ISO 9000** family of standards, probably the most important set of standards ever issued.

2 Types of standards

If you wrote out a detailed plan for a well-organized working day in your current job it might contain tasks such as 'Get the 8:07 train', 'Print out reports for 11am monthly meeting with Mrs Grimaldi', and the like.

If you wrote out a plan for a well-organized working day that **anyone** could use you would have to generalize the items specific to your job: 'Make sure you arrive on time', 'Anticipate and prepare for the day's events', and so on.

Likewise some standards are highly specific to particular products, while others are more generally applicable to ways of organizing work.

2.1 Product standards

The vast majority of standards set out requirements for particular types of product. Here are some random examples from the BSI online catalogue (the BSI claims that its library contains over half a million standards!).

- Hexalobular socket cheese head screws (BS EN ISO 14580:2001)
- Dental tweezers. General requirements (BS EN ISO 15098–1:2001)
- Concrete. Specification, performance, production and conformity (BS EN 206–1:2000)
- Optical fibre cables. Generic specification. General (BS EN 60794–1–1:2002)

If you **make** such products then your organization will probably have copies of the product standards that are relevant to your work. If your organization **buys** such products then it may well be part of purchasing policy that you only buy products that conform to the necessary product standards.

2.2 Systems standards

A system is something that takes **inputs** and performs **processes** on those inputs to produce **outputs**. A bread-making system takes flour and yeast and water (inputs), mixes them up, kneads the mixture, proves it, bakes it (processes), and produces loaves of bread (outputs).

Any aspect of work can be seen in this way, too. In fact, an organization as a whole can be seen as a system, made up of lots of smaller interrelated systems.

Activity 6

15 mins

S/NVQ A1.3

This Activity is the second of a series of three which together may provide the basis of appropriate evidence for your S/NVQ portfolio. The others are Activities 4 and 20. If you are intending to take this course of action, it might be better to write your answers on separate sheets of paper.

Describe the work of your own work team as a system, in other words in terms of inputs, processes and outputs. An input is any kind of resource, for instance the time taken by you and your colleagues to do various activities. You don't need to list every paper clip, but be as specific and detailed as necessary to enable a new recruit to have a good overview of what your job involves.

Systems standards set out requirements for the good organization and management of processes. For instance, if an organization can prove that it complies with BS EN ISO 14001 *Environmental Management Systems,* then anybody buying goods or services from that organization can be assured that it will carry out all its work processes in an environmentally friendly way.

As we have said, the most important systems standards are the ones that make up the BS EN ISO 9000 *Quality Management Systems* family of standards.

3 BS EN ISO 9000:2000

3.1 The BS EN ISO 9000 'family'

The term 'BS EN ISO 9000' (often abbreviated to ISO 9000) usually refers to a **family** of quality management systems standards. The latest versions were published at the end of 2000.

The family includes four principal standards.

■ ISO 9000:2000. *Quality management systems. Fundamentals and vocabulary.* This describes basic concepts and specifies the terminology for quality management systems.

■ ISO 9001:2000. *Quality management systems. Requirements.* This specifies the requirements for a quality management system where an organization needs to demonstrate its ability to provide products that fulfil customer and applicable regulatory requirements and aim to enhance customer satisfaction.

If an organization wishes to obtain independent certification of its quality system it will be audited and assessed according to the requirements set out here.

EXTENSION 2
To see the requirements for ISO 9000:2000 registration, see David Hoyle's *ISO 9000 Quality Systems Handbook*

■ ISO 9004:2000. *Quality management systems. Guidelines for performance improvements.* This is a more detailed version of ISO 9001:2000: it includes (word for word) all the key sections of ISO 9001:2000 but it adds further notes explaining the requirements in more detail and giving examples. It is meant to be used for guidance purposes, not for certification.

■ ISO 19011. *Guidelines on Quality and/or Environmental Management Systems Auditing.* This is under development at the time of writing. It will provide guidance on how to audit quality management systems and environmental management systems.

3.2 Key concepts

■ **Customer focus**
We have stressed that the starting point for quality is in the wants and needs of customers and this is very much recognized in the ISO 9000:2000 family. ISO 9000 states from the outset that the **purpose** of a quality management system is to assist organizations to enhance customer satisfaction.

This means finding out and understanding customer needs, and then at least meeting those needs and, preferably, exceeding expectations.

■ **Continuous improvement**
The standards also recognize that in the modern world, with its ever-increasing competitive pressures and technological advances, customers' needs and expectations will constantly change. Great emphasis is therefore placed on **continuous improvement** of products and processes.

This means that the organization should engage in a constant cycle of analyzing the existing situation to identify areas for improvement, seeking possible solutions, and then measuring results once the chosen solutions have been implemented to ensure that things really have improved.

■ **Top management leadership and involvement**
Quality management systems should be initiated and championed by the most senior management in the organization. They should promote the quality objectives to ensure that all staff are aware of them and are involved in implementing them. They should ensure that any resources that are needed

are available and they should keep the quality management system under constant review.

■ **A process approach**

The ISO 9000 family takes the view that if an organization is to operate effectively it needs to identify and manage a large number of linked activities. Work activities (processes) use resources and transform them into outputs. The output from one process often forms the input into another.

This 'process approach' is seen as the best way of achieving control over the linkage between individual processes and ensuring that they combine and interact effectively.

■ **Products and product realization**

The ISO 9000 family uses the term 'product' in a broader sense than you might be used to. A product is the 'result of a process' and there are four generic product categories.

■ Services (for example, a restaurant)
■ Software (for example, a dictionary or a computer program)
■ Hardware (for example, a mechanical part)
■ Processed materials (for example, lubricant)

Many products are actually a combination of one or more categories. A car, for instance, is a combination of all four of these categories.

Product realization is another important term, as we shall see later. This refers to the interconnected processes that are used to bring products into being. A product starts out as an idea which is then realized by following a set of product realization processes.

Activity 7

4 mins

Think about your organization's products. Which of the four generic product categories do they fit in to?

_____

_____

_____

_____

3.3 Certification under ISO 9001

Organizations may decide that they need to develop a quality management system that meets the ISO 9000 family of standards for a variety of reasons.

- Because they feel the need to control or improve the quality of their products.
- To reduce costs, or become more competitive.
- Because customers expect them to do so.
- Because they want to supply products to a government body that refuses to do business with organizations unless their quality management systems are independently verified.

In the last two examples it would clearly be helpful to be able to produce **proof of compliance** with the standards and this is available in the form of a certificate.

If an organization were certified under the 1994 version of ISO 9001 and wanted to retain ISO 9001 certification it would have until 15 December 2003 to convert its systems to comply with the new standard.

To become certified the organization has to develop a quality management system that meets the **requirements** specified by **ISO 9001:2000**. (Note that ISO 9000 and ISO 9004 are guidelines, not requirements.)

Once the quality system has been fully developed and implemented, the organization must ask an independent Registrar to audit it. Registrars are organizations who are accredited to issue ISO 9001 certificates by the United Kingdom Accreditation Service (UKAS). After the audit, all being well, the Registrar will issue an official certificate and potential customers will accept this as proof of compliance with ISO 9001.

3.4 ISO 9001:2000 in outline

ISO 9001:2000 has three introductory sections and then sets out its requirements under five main headings.

Section(s)	
1–3	Introductory
4	Quality management system
5	Management responsibility
6	Resource management
7	Product realization
8	Measurement, analysis and improvement

In the remainder of this session we are going to look in some depth at the requirements of ISO 9001:2000. The numbering of the remaining sections and headings in this Session (Sections 4, 5, 6, 7 and 8) corresponds exactly to that used in the standard.

4 Quality management system

4.1 General requirements

An organization should identify and describe the **processes** that it wants to make up its quality system, and then use and manage those processes. The performance of the system should be monitored and improved where necessary.

For example, if your staff regularly write letters to customers you probably expect them to do a spell check before they send their letters. But maybe they forget sometimes: we all do!

Under ISO 9001 your department's letter-writing would first be identified as part of a process. The **description** of this part of the process would include the requirement to spell check all letters. An **improvement** to the process might be a software modification that automatically forced a spell check, before you printed out any letter for posting.

4.2 Documentation requirements

Quality system documents consist of a quality manual, forms and checklists, external documents such as government regulations or customer specifications, and records such as accounting records, timesheets, production schedules, correspondence – anything, in fact, that provides evidence of the processes being carried out.

In a modern organization it is unlikely that paper 'documents' will be printed. The organization's intranet is the ideal home for such documentation.

Quality manual (4.2.1)

In a complex organization the quality manual may be a very large and detailed document. It defines the scope of the quality system, documents all of its processes and describes how they interact.

Note that the manual should explain how processes interact. This is a crucial point. Although you may not need to know in detail how every other part of your organization does its work, you must always remember that what you do has an impact on other parts of the organization. If you are late with something, you cause delays in the department that deals with the next stage of getting the product to the customer.

Activity 8 · 4 mins

Your organization contracts out office cleaning to a specialist third-party company. Are that cleaning company's processes within the scope of your company's quality system, or can they be ignored completely? Justify your answer.

_____

_____

_____

_____

_____

Your organization's quality system may well include a requirement for you and your staff not to make unnecessary mess, in the interests of efficient working and health and safety, and to keep cleaning costs down. But the detailed processes carried out by a third-party cleaning company are beyond the scope of your organization's quality system.

Control of documents (4.2.2)

Any procedural guidelines that are developed and any documents that are used over and over again should be subject to controls, to make sure that everyone is using the 'official' and up-to-date version.

For instance, a set of guidelines might have the following just after the title.

Version	1.2
Date of issue	14 May 2004
Approved by	Susan Grimaldi, Marketing Director
Approved on	13 May 2004
Version history	
1.2	14/05/04: updated for changes announced in the Budget 2004
1.1	27/09/03: updated to reflect changes in accounting software
1.0	05/06/03: initial release

A single page document such as a form or a checklist might have a header or a footer giving (at the very least) the version number.

If **external** documents, such as statutory rules or a precise set of customer specifications, have to be followed, it is equally important that the **latest version** is used.

In both cases, of course, everyone involved should be told when a new version is available to make sure that they don't accidentally follow obsolete procedures.

Activity 9

3 mins

How could an intranet help with control of quality documents?

_____

_____

_____

_____

_____

If quality documents are held on an intranet staff will always have the very latest versions instantly available. Even if they print out a document for convenience they can easily and quickly check for updates. Lengthy documents will be easily searchable. Documents can contain links to official sources of external documents, for instance government websites. Announcements about new versions of documents (or any other quality issue) can be found by consulting the home page, rather than having to search for an e-mail or memo that might have been sent out several weeks earlier. You may have had additional ideas.

Control of records (4.2.3)

Records are the main source of evidence that quality requirements have been met. If your organization promises delivery within one working day then your records should prove that customers who placed orders on Monday received their goods on Tuesday.

Records can be in any form, but they should be legible if they are hand-written, and they should be easily retrievable when needed, for instance if there is a dispute about what the customer ordered, or if an auditor asks to see them to check that the system is working properly.

Business and taxation law sets out statutory rules about keeping certain documents (such as invoices), but the quality management system will probably go further.

For instance, if customers start returning products it will be helpful to have detailed internal production records that enable individual products to be traced to the particular machine that made them. Or if a certain customer makes an unusual number of repeat orders it could be helpful to keep internal records that show which staff member in customer services deals with that customer: he or she is obviously doing something that ought to be adopted more widely!

Activity 10

3 mins

Your organization promises delivery within one working day. What records would need to be kept to prove to a quality system auditor that your organization fulfils its delivery guarantee?

_____

_____

_____

_____

_____

_____

As a minimum the auditor would want to see copies of customers' orders, documents relating to the despatch of products from your premises, and delivery notes, signed by the customer and noting the time of delivery. Auditors would also look for any correspondence relating to delivery issues, contracts with carrier companies and/or instructions to delivery staff.

5 Management responsibility

On your own initiative, after reading this Session, you might decide to implement a quality management system in your own department. That's fine, but unless all the other departments that you deal with do likewise the chances are that your efforts will have little overall effect.

The initiative needs to come from the very top of the organization and be communicated to everyone within the organization. A positive attitude towards quality management needs to be so deeply ingrained that it is an expectation: something so fundamental that staff would never even consider approaching their work in any other way.

5.1 Management commitment

Top management should be heavily involved in the quality management system and give it their unqualified support.

Case histories show that good initiatives in organizations often fail because of lack of commitment from the principal decision makers.

For instance, top managers may encourage early attempts to implement a quality management system but not be willing to provide resources (people, time, new equipment) to maintain the system, in the longer term. Or, as a quick fix, in a crisis they may endorse activities that undermine the quality policy.

ISO 9001 therefore stipulates that such managers should be involved in formulating quality policy and objectives (see below), they should actively promote the importance of quality throughout the organization and they should periodically perform quality management reviews and provide whatever resources are needed for maintenance of the system and further improvement.

5.2 Customer focus

As we have said repeatedly, customer focus is about identifying customer requirements, meeting those requirements and enhancing customer satisfaction.

ISO 9001 says that top management should approach their own work with these aims in mind and they should expect everyone in their organization to do likewise.

Activity 11

3 mins

Why might an organization lose its customer focus? Try to think of at least two reasons.

_____

_____

_____

_____

An organization may get complacent about customers if it is the only or market-leading supplier of a certain product because it does not have the pressure of competition.

An organization may be led by people whose main motivation is the pleasure they get from making products, whether or not customers actually want lots of innovative new features that only appear to show off how clever the makers are.

An organization may simply neglect to collect and analyze feedback from customers on a regular enough basis. Or it may be slack about monitoring the actions of competitors.

5.3 Quality policy

A policy is a plan or a course of action. For instance it may be 'government policy' to ensure that nursery school places are available for all children aged 2 to 4 years old. A policy sets out what is to be achieved, but it does not say in detail how it will be achieved.

ISO 9001 says that management should devise a quality policy and ensure that it is appropriate to their organization's purpose. It should emphasize the need to meet quality requirements and make a commitment to continuous improvement. It should facilitate the development of quality objectives (see below). It should be communicated and understood throughout the organization and it should be reviewed regularly to ensure that it is still suitable.

Some organizations' policies are very brief. For example:

We practice continuous improvement to achieve customer delight by providing customer-centric, cost-effective, timely and qualitative software solutions.

Note that this is nevertheless 'appropriate' in the sense that it specifies 'software solutions'.

Others may be more elaborate.

XYZ Ltd – Quality Policy

At XYZ Ltd we are dedicated to achieving the highest degree of Customer (internal and external) satisfaction!

We will achieve this by:

- Knowing who our Customers are and what they want – through open communication.
- Understanding the requirements of our jobs and the systems that support us – through training and education.
- Making continuous improvement a part of every day and every job – through the use of team participation and measurements.
- Ensuring that our Policy and Procedure Manuals reflect what we actually do.
- Remembering that we are here because of our Customers. Realizing our Customers are the reason we have our jobs, and that providing on-time delivery of quality parts at a fair market price is how we will keep them.
- Helping each other to help ourselves.
- Understanding how our jobs fit into the overall flow of work at XYZ Ltd.

C   Continuous Improvement through
A   Alignment of our Missions and Goals
R   Responsibility and Respect for our job and each other
E   Educating one another

5.4 Planning

Quality objectives (5.4.1)

Objectives set out how a plan will be achieved. They should be Specific, Measurable, Achievable, Relevant, and Time bound (SMART). For example:

> 'To set up a database showing details of places available at all nursery schools in the UK by July 2004.'

ISO 9001 requires management to ensure that appropriate and measurable objectives are set for all functional areas and at all organizational levels.

Activity 12

3 mins

See if you can write a SMART objective relevant to XYZ Ltd's goal that staff should understand the requirements of their jobs and the systems that support them – through training and education.

_____

_____

_____

_____

_____

_____

Here is a possible answer.

> 'To provide all customer services staff with one hour's instruction (including a quiz to test understanding) each month on the benefits for customers of new features in the 2004 range of parts'.

Many other answers are possible – as long as they are SMART.

Quality management system planning (5.4.2)

This requirement needs no elaboration except to say that it makes it clear that it is top management's responsibility to plan a quality management system such as that described in Section 4 of ISO 9001and make sure that it continues to work effectively and is improved where possible.

5.5 Responsibility, authority and communication

We'll shift our perspective for a moment to discuss this set of requirements, and think about what an ISO 9001 auditor might be looking for as **evidence** that an organization was complying with them.

Responsibility and authority (5.5.1)

Requirement	Management should define, clarify and communicate responsibilities and authorities for people whose work affects quality.
Possible evidence	Clearly labelled organization charts showing who reports to whom; job descriptions; employment contracts; noticeboards; newsletters; e-mails; intranet content.

Management representative (5.5.2)

Requirement	Management should appoint a person to oversee the quality management system, report on the status of the system and support its improvement.
Possible evidence	Evidence of the appointment, discussions with the management representative about his or her job; review of written reports and action taken in response to them; resources available to the management representative (support staff, information systems etc.); evidence of changes to the system over time; liaison with the registration agency.

Ensure promotion of awareness of customer requirements throughout the organization (5.5.3)

Requirement	Management should ensure that internal communication processes are established and that communication occurs throughout the organization.
Possible evidence	'Staff suggestion' procedures, noticeboards, newsletters, e-mails, intranet content, memos, manuals and so on; interviews with staff to ascertain their level of awareness of quality issues within the organization; actions taken in response to suggestions from staff.

5.6 Management review

General (5.6.1)

As you have probably noticed, a number of requirements stress the point that the quality management system should be kept under review. In most organizations this is probably done via a monthly or quarterly meeting of directors and other managers at which performance to date is discussed, and ideas for improvements are presented and approved.

Review input (5.6.2)

The meeting or other review process is likely to have a regular agenda of matters to discuss, or 'inputs'.

Activity 13 · 4 mins

See if you can draw up an agenda for such a meeting.

_____

_____

_____

_____

_____

_____

_____

_____

_____

_____

_____

_____

_____

_____

Here's a suggestion, based on the inputs listed in ISO 9001.

XYZ LTD QUALITY STEERING COMMITTEE

MEETING ON 31 MAY 2004 AT 10:30 AM

AGENDA

1 Matters arising from previous meeting
2 Consideration of reports from internal or external quality audits
3 Feedback from customers
4 Review of process performance
5 Review of product conformity data
6 Review of corrective and preventive actions taken
7 Consideration of changes that might affect the system (new government regulations, new customer specifications, etc.)
8 Recommendations for improvement

Review output (5.6.3)

Outputs from the review process should be **decisions and actions** that will improve the quality system, improve products so that they better meet customer requirements; and obtain whatever resources will be needed to achieve this.

6 Resource management

6.1 Quality resources

To meet the requirements of Section 6 of ISO 9001 the organization must be able to show that it has identified and provided the resources needed to implement, maintain and improve the quality system and to enhance customer satisfaction.

This means people, the place where they work and the things that they work with.

6.2 Human resources

General (6.2.1)

Everybody in the organization may affect quality in some way, but some people's work will have a more direct impact than others. An organization's staff should have the **right** experience, education, training and skills to do the job that they do.

In many jobs this is self-evident, for instance a law firm is unlikely to appoint a new solicitor without checking that the person has appropriate legal qualifications. It is unlikely to ask an expert in conveyancing to handle a murder case.

Sometimes it is less obvious, for instance it might not seem necessary to train the law firm's receptionist when a new piece of legislation is enacted, but if a customer calls and asks to speak to an expert on that new legislation it would be helpful if the receptionist at least knew who to put the call through to.

The law firm should ensure that its receptionists are trained in such matters to the extent that they can interpret customers' enquiries and handle them appropriately.

Competence, awareness and training (6.2.2)

The organization should define acceptable levels of **competence** for each job, and maintain **records of competence** (typically this would be part of an individual's personnel record.)

In some cases external measures may be used to help define competence. For instance, trainee accountants are promoted to positions with more responsibility as they pass annual exams set by an accounting body.

More often, competence is expressed in terms such as 'able to motivate team members', 'able to meet deadlines' and the like, and these things are best judged by assessing performance in the job.

In either case the organization needs to be able to show the quality auditors that it takes measures to identify individuals' **training needs** and then delivers training programmes to meet those needs: For example, an in-house course for new First Line Managers on motivation or time management, or a day-release scheme for accountants to study at a college,

The organization also needs to evaluate the effectiveness of training. For example, if people continue to miss deadlines after going on a time management course, perhaps there is another reason for the problem such as insufficient knowledge of the system, or perhaps something not related to training at all.

The **awareness** requirement is partly a matter of communicating the quality policy and quality objectives throughout the organization, as we saw earlier, but for individuals it may be necessary to make certain that people understand how specific aspects of their work contribute to quality objectives.

Activity 14

3 mins

A call centre has a policy of giving all callers a reference number at the end of a call, in case of further enquiries.

A staff member taking a straightforward call knows from experience that he has handled it as thoroughly as possible, and that no further enquiries will arise. Therefore he does not bother to allocate a number to that caller.

Assuming that no further enquiries arise in this case, does it matter that no reference number was allocated? Explain your answer.

_____

_____

_____

_____

When procedures are very complex, and require different inputs from many different people, it can be very difficult for individuals to see the reason for doing things in a certain order or for maintaining certain records.

The number allocated may be used for a number of purposes (other than making it easier for difficult callers to phone up again and be more difficult!). For example, it may be part of a system that measures the length of time taken on different types of calls. If certain types of calls become more frequent, then the organization may need to allocate more resources to deal with them. By not recording this call the individual may inadvertently be helping to deprive his department of resources that it will need in the future.

When members of staff question the value of doing some part of their job, therefore, it is never acceptable to say 'We do it because that's what it says in the manual'. The explanation needs to be given in terms of how that task helps with other tasks. (If it doesn't, the procedure should be changed!)

6.3 Infrastructure

ISO 9001 requires organizations to identify, provide for and maintain **infrastructure needs**.

Infrastructure consists of:

- buildings, workspace and associated utilities;
- hardware/equipment;
- software (this means reference books as well as computer programs);
- support services (for instance, the internal telephone system, the fleet of delivery vehicles).

The Super Series books *Preventing Accidents* and *Managing Lawfully – Health, Safety and Environment* have more information about safe infrastructure and environment at work.

In the UK many of these things are governed by Health and Safety at Work legislation. For instance there are specific rules about how much space a person should have, what sort of seats they should have, and so on. There are minimum standards for display screens, so as to avoid eye strain. Untidiness can become a safety or hygiene hazard as well as a cause of inefficiency.

Activity 15

3 mins

Imagine you are conducting a quality management systems audit. What type of evidence would you look for to assess the adequacy of 'software'?

_____

_____

_____

_____

_____

_____

Clearly the precise 'software' required varies considerably, depending on the type of organization and the type of tasks being done. Ideally the auditors should be sufficiently acquainted with the organization's industry to know, or be able to find out, what the standard reference works are and which computer applications are considered 'Best of Breed'.

An organization may have perfectly legitimate reasons for not using such products, but the auditors would want to know what those reasons were. They would want to know whether there were any consequences that compromised quality, such as: lack of compatibility with other systems or other organizations; duplicated work; work that could be automated; inability to analyze information outputs, and so on.

More generally the auditors could glean evidence by observing staff who were using the software. They might ask individuals whether they found it a help or a hindrance in getting their job done, and look for evidence of system failures caused by the software used.

6.4　Work environment

This requirement says that the organization should identify and manage **work environment** factors needed to ensure that its products meet quality requirements.

There is some overlap with infrastructure here: for instance the lighting, temperature and décor might be considered part of the environment as well as part of the infrastructure.

Some aspects of the work environment are merely practical: for example, people whose work needs quiet concentration should not be expected to work in areas that have constantly ringing telephones or where there is noise from machinery.

Some aspects are social, psychological and cultural: auditors might be able to observe whether staff willingly co-operate with their colleagues, and can ask them, say, if they feel that they are given enough freedom, or a host of other questions. Of course, there are no right answers that apply to all organizations: different environments suit different companies.

Every year *The Sunday Times* publishes a list of the '100 Best Companies to Work For'.

This is measured on the basis of employees' responses to a questionnaire, which evaluates: trust in management, pride in work and company, staff satisfaction, camaraderie, company structure, ownership, employees' benefits, internal communications, and recognition schemes.

7 Product realization

A product starts out as an **idea** which is then **made real** by following a set of **product realization processes**.

This exclusion clause is a new feature in ISO 9000:2000. The 1994 version was far more rigid and prescriptive. The new version means that quality systems can be much better tailored to particular organizations and yet still achieve certification.

Remember that 'product' in the ISO 9000 context means services, software, hardware or processed materials. Because of the huge variety of possible products and methods of realizing them the ISO allows organizations to **ignore or exclude** any requirement in Section 7 if they cannot apply it because of the nature of the organization or the nature of the product.

For example, one requirement in Section 7 concerns calibration of monitoring and measuring devices. This would be highly relevant in a manufacturing business, but rather less so in a firm of solicitors: it would be absurd to take this requirement so far that all staff synchronize watches at the start of each day!

7.1 Planning of product realization

This is a general requirement to plan and develop product realization processes in the light of the organization's quality objectives and its customers' requirements.

Planning will include devising product realization documents and record-keeping systems, and methods to control quality during product realization.

7.2 Customer-related processes

Determination of requirements related to the product (7.2.1)

Requirements related to the product need to be considered from three points of view: the customer, any relevant external body, and the organization itself.

As you know, the customer is considered first: your organization may be able to make very good blue size 5 widgets but if customers only want green size 3 widgets there is no point in 'realizing' the larger blue ones.

External bodies may set legal requirements or industry standards that your product has to meet. Obviously you can't ignore these because you cannot sell illegal products and you want to be at least as good as the competition.

Your organization's own requirements cannot be ignored. For instance, although the customer may not care if your product bears your company logo and contact details, it is likely to be a very good idea for your organization's marketing purposes. Perhaps the most important organizational requirement is cost: you may be able to produce what a customer wants, but not at a profit. As a one-off this may be a worthwhile gesture of goodwill, but your company will soon be bankrupt if it ignores the organizational requirement to cover its costs.

Review of requirements related to the product (7.2.2)

Whenever an organization commits itself to providing a product it should be sure that the customer's requirements are fully defined and understood and that the organization has the ability to meet those requirements.

Requirements will, of course, change from time to time and appropriate records should be kept of new instructions, negotiations, and contract changes.

Customer communication (7.2.3)

The organization should establish effective communications with the customer to ensure that product information is available and that there are suitable channels for enquiries, feedback and complaints.

For a typical modern organization this means (at the very least) that there should be customer service staff answering telephones, sending out product information on request and dealing with written correspondence. In addition a website is now almost obligatory: this can show product information in detail, provide e-mail links for enquiries and allow customers to view the current status of their orders.

Activity 16

3 mins

A surprising number of websites do not give 'ordinary' contact information such as the company's address and telephone number, or they make such information hard to find. Why do you think this might be?

_____

_____

_____

_____

In some cases it is just bad website design. Most Web design gurus say that the address and phone number should be shown on the first page of a website and preferably on all the other pages.

The truth in many cases (particularly in the case of Internet start-up companies), is that the company does not want to be contacted by telephone or letter because it does not employ resources to deal with such contacts. This situation is only justifiable if the company's Internet-based customer service is so good that non-Internet methods of contact are never necessary. Few, if any, companies yet come close to this ideal.

7.3 Design and development

ISO 9001 has **seven requirements** under this heading. Remember that we are talking about product **realization** – taking an initial idea and turning it into something that the customer wants – and that a 'product' need not be a physical product.

The **first four requirements** are listed below. As ever, records should be kept in all cases to enable the organization to keep control of the process, identify where improvements can be made and as evidence for auditors.

Design and development planning (7.3.1)
Design and development inputs (7.3.2)
Design and development outputs (7.3.3)
Design and development review (7.3.4)

Even the best ideas will just be wishes, and not be realized at all, unless **plans** are made. There should be a timetable defining the stages of design and development (preferably with specific deadlines). Specific individuals should be given the responsibility to achieve specific things (**outputs**), and they should be given whatever authority they need to command the resources (**inputs**) they will need.

A large or complex product may need the involvement of many different parts of the organization, and external organizations will probably be needed to supply materials or expertise that is not available in-house. Design and development planning should identify all the interested parties, consider how they will interact, and make arrangements to ensure that everyone will have the information they need to do their part of the job.

If the organization has designed and developed similar products before then everything may go exactly to plan. But plans need not be set in stone: they should be flexible enough to allow for changes. There may be unanticipated problems, particularly if the idea is a totally new one; or the design and development process itself may give rise to further good ideas, which were not part of the original plan but are worth incorporating.

There are limits, of course. A product may never be realized if the release date is constantly put off to accommodate each and every new idea. For this reason it is sensible to appoint a specific person or group of people who will **review** and approve each stage of the design, and sign it off so that it passes on to the next stage. Likewise, changes should also be subject to approval: some suggested changes may not get approval if they would delay the product too much.

The **fifth and sixth requirements** use terminology that needs a little explanation.

Design and development verification (7.3.5)

'**Verification**' in ISO 9001 means checking to see whether the outputs from the design process meet the **organization's** design goals.
This may sound self-evident, but it is all too easy to get carried away by the creative design and development process and forget some of the original aims or requirements. Alternatively, corners may have been cut to keep the project on schedule. Verification should be done on an ongoing basis, perhaps at each 'approval' stage, and consider issues such as whether the product still complies with safety standards, whether, after all the innovations and changes, it is still compatible with other products that the organization has on the market, and so on.

Design and development validation (7.3.6)

'**Validation**' means checking to see whether the product does what the **customer** or user wants it to do under real-world conditions.

Again, it is easy to lose sight of this fundamental requirement during the design and development process. The organization can go back to its original list of customer needs and tick them off if the product seems to fulfil them, but by far the best way to check is to ask potential buyers to test the product and make sure that they give plenty of feedback.

Control of development changes (7.3.7)

The **seventh and final requirement** is one that we have mentioned already in the discussion above: the organization should identify, record, review and verify changes in product design and development and make sure that they are approved before they are implemented.

7.4 Purchasing

Purchasing process (7.4.1)

ISO 9001 says that organizations should establish criteria for selecting, evaluating and re-evaluating suppliers and purchased products and services. One way of doing this, of course, is to insist that your suppliers themselves are certified under ISO 9001!

This may not always be appropriate, though. The level of controls over suppliers should be based on the type of purchased item, its impact on the final product, and the supplier's past performance. For instance, if your product needs a motor and motors are supplied by Z Limited then there should be close controls over Z Limited. But if you add a few drops of oil to the motor, as part of your production process, it is probably far less important to micro-manage your oil supplier.

Many organizations, particularly very large ones, have their own 'preferred supplier' schemes, requiring potential suppliers to meet rigorous industry-specific standards. One example is Boeing's policy, which you can see on www.boeing.com/company offices/doingbiz/psc/home.htm

Purchasing information (7.4.2)

This requirement relates to purchasing documentation. Documentation should clearly describe the products or services being purchased and include details of whatever specifications are appropriate: size, colour, format, length and so on. If this information is spelled out in detail it is easier for purchasing staff to buy the right items and easier for suppliers to supply them.

Verification of purchased product (7.4.3)

This requirement simply states that the organization should verify purchased products before they use them. For instance, if you buy flour to make bread you should make sure that it is not full of weevils **before** adding it to the mix.

We'll be looking at ways of sampling purchased products to test quality in Session D of this book.

Activity 17

3 mins

What does 'verify' mean in an ISO 9001 context?

_____

_____

_____

If you are not sure, you should be able to answer this question by looking back at the previous section.

7.5 Production and service provision

Having designed and developed the product (7.3) and bought in all the supplies needed (7.4), this section deals with the actual production processes. Remember that organizations only need to adhere to Section 7 requirements of ISO 9001 if they are relevant.

Control of production and service provision (7.5.1)

The organization should carry out production and service processes under 'controlled' conditions. Here are some examples of controls.

- Information that describes the product should be available.
- Work instructions should set out how the product is made.
- Any equipment used should be suitable for the job.
- Monitoring and measuring devices should be available and properly used.

Auditors will also be looking not only for evidence of authorization to release the product for dispatch, but also for evidence that there are controls over product delivery and post-delivery activities.

Validation of processes for production and service provision (7.5.2)

This requirement refers in particular to 'special processes'. A 'special' process is any process where it is impractical or unsafe to perform tests and inspections during the actual process. Usually the quality of the work can only be fully validated by destructive testing or prolonged use of the product.

Examples include baking, heat treatments, coatings, concrete mixing, soldering, welding, painting, gluing. The only practical way of testing a loaf of bread is to eat it. The only way test how long a non-stick frying pan lasts is to use it until the non-stick coating fails. So how can such processes be validated?

In this situation the organization needs to develop special work instructions or procedures that verify the materials and process input (temperature, equipment speed, and so on) **before** the process begins and then check **samples** of the product output once the process is complete.

Prolonged use of some items (such as non-stick frying pans) can be **simulated** in laboratories. Car safety is simulated using crash-test dummies. Loaves of bread are tested using a combination of consumer panels (who taste the bread) and sampling and statistical process control (which uses the laws of probability to make sure that all batches of loaves are produced to the same standard). We'll discuss statistical process control in Session D of this book.

Note that this validation requirement also applies to all other processes, and to process personnel and process equipment.

Activity 18 · 4 mins

What does 'validate' mean in the context of ISO 9001 and how could you validate service provision processes in a hairdressers?

_____

_____

_____

_____

As we saw earlier, validation means checking to see whether the product does what the customer or user wants it to do under real-world conditions.

In a hairdressing salon you would need to have controls over the hairdressers you employed – make sure that they are properly qualified and have appropriate experience. Hairdressers often offer special deals to customers who are willing to have their hair cut by a trainee. The customer's reaction on seeing the finished haircut is a form of validation.

Identification and traceability (7.5.3)

Some products are tailored to specific customers. For instance a firm of printers might produce a range of invoice stationery with standard layouts, but each batch would have a different company's logo, address and VAT details. Or you might produce a version of your product in a non-standard shape, size or colour at the request of a specific customer.

If your organization does this kind of work, ISO 9001 requires you to establish, maintain and record the identity and status of products throughout production, from the time the raw materials are received and during all stages of production, delivery and installation.

Customer property (7.5.4)

This is similar to the previous requirement, with the additional proviso that when the customer provides something that your organization uses in the production process, it should be carefully safeguarded. If you take your car to a dealer to have a new radio fitted, then you also expect the dealer to take care of your car. If you supply a sofa manufacturer with some fabric that you bought on an exotic holiday, then you would expect the manufacturer to return any unused offcuts to you, together with the sofa.

Other examples include building or installation work in the customer's premises and even intellectual property such as ideas.

Preservation of product (7.5.5)

This requirement simply says that the organization should prevent damage or deterioration to the product during handling, processing, storage, packaging and delivery.

7.6 Control of monitoring and measuring devices

This requirement is about **monitoring and measuring of product realization processes** as opposed to monitoring and measuring of the quality management system as a whole, which is dealt with in Section 8 (below).

Practically all physical products need to conform to size, shape, weight or volume requirements. If your organization claims to produce 2 cm tap washers those washers should measure 2 cm, otherwise they will not fit into the taps they are intended for. If you produce a packet that says it contains 3 kg of potatoes you should make sure that it contains at least 3 kg otherwise you are breaking the law.

This requirement says that you should identify the monitoring and measuring that needs to be done; select devices (weights, meters, computer software and so on) that meet those monitoring and measuring needs; and protect them from unauthorized adjustment, damage or deterioration.

Equipment should regularly be 'calibrated', which means that its operation should be checked against a standard measure. For example, you may have a device that is set to cut materials into 30 cm lengths. To make sure that the machine is correctly calibrated you check that the lengths are indeed 30 cm long, using something that is not part of the machine, such as a ruler.

8 Measurement, analysis and improvement

8.1 General

In broad terms Section 8 of ISO 9001 is about 'remedial processes'. The requirements are intended to ensure that the organization makes the effort to find out whether it is conforming to its quality objectives and takes appropriate action if not.

8.2 Monitoring and measurement

Customer satisfaction (8.2.1)

Under this heading organizations are firstly required to identify ways to monitor and measure customer satisfaction – and then actually do so and **use** the customer satisfaction information.

As we've stressed from the outset of this book, the ultimate test of the quality management system is whether it results in satisfied customers. But how do you know if your customers are satisfied?

Customers will often let you know if they are **not** satisfied. They will phone up or write in, demanding that you put things right. But this does not always happen. Sometimes a dissatisfied customer will just make a mental note not to buy anything from you ever again.

Satisfied customers will rarely let you know that they are satisfied, and why should they? They have a right to expect to be satisfied.

Activity 19

3 mins

Suggest three ways of finding out whether or not customers are satisfied with the quality of your product, assuming they don't tell you voluntarily, for instance by complaining.

_____

_____

_____

_____

_____

_____

_____

Here are some answers. You may well have had other ideas.

- If you know exactly who your customers are then you may be able to phone them up and ask them. This can easily be done if you sell directly to other businesses or if you sell high-value items like cars or new kitchen installations, but it is not practicable for high-volume retail items sold to the general public (baked beans, for instance).

- You can include a feedback mechanism with the product: a number to ring, a form to fill in or a website address. The drawback is that there is little incentive to fill it in unless the customer has particularly strong feelings about the product. Some companies try to encourage responses with prize draws and the like.

- You can set up focus groups and invite a sample of typical consumers to visit your premises, try out your products and give their opinions. This is a more suitable approach for high-volume retail items. A variation on this is the random interview, conducted by stopping people on the high street or knocking on doors.

- You can employ a market research organization: they use a wide variety of methods to test opinion of your product.

- You can monitor the general media or publications specific to your industry. Consumer magazines like _Which_ conduct independent comparative studies and give 'Best Buy' awards.

- Sales figures give some indication, but should not be considered in isolation. An apparent leap in sales may be because a competitor product was temporarily unavailable, not because customers like your product.

Internal audit (8.2.2)

An 'audit' is an investigation to determine whether a system's processes, checks and controls are working properly and the system is doing what it is supposed to do.

As we've seen, a third party registrar will conduct an independent 'external' audit of your entire quality management system, but one of the things he or she will be looking for is evidence that your organization carries out its own regular 'internal' audits and that any problems discovered during audits are solved.

Large organizations often have a separate team of internal auditors who have a cycle of work throughout the year investigating different departments.

Auditors devise audit 'programmes' (detailed checklists) and develop methods to verify the system they are checking, often using **statistical sampling techniques** (see Sessions C and D).

For example, if your department's procedures manual states that certain documents should be approved by the head or assistant head of department before it is released, then the following question may appear in the internal audit programme.

Test 15.3.1	Yes	No	Method	Comment
Is daily document X approved, before release, by the head of department?	✔		Check 20 random samples against list of authorized signatures	One exception

The programme would be backed up by documentary evidence that the test had been performed. In this case the audit file would contain a copy of the list of authorized signatures and details of the specific items checked. An extract from the backing evidence, to show that the test had been performed using the proper method, might look like this.

Date	Signature	Authorized signatory?	Comments/Action
13/02/2004	JBG	Yes	
18/02/2004	MPJ	Yes	
23/02/2004			Not authorized. Validity checked with JBG and confirmed during audit.
27/02/2004	JBG	Yes	

Note that the auditor cannot simply tick the list without checking properly. He or she has to find and check the actual document, making a note who of signed it, whether the signature matches the sample on the list of authorized signatories, and has to follow the matter up if there are any discrepancies.

Monitoring and measurement of processes (8.2.3)

This requirement says that the organization should use suitable methods to monitor and measure its **processes** and take action when the processes fail to achieve planned results.

Obviously the way in which this is applied will vary enormously, depending on the process in question and what its planned result is.

Activity 20

30 mins

Portfolio of evidence

S/NVQ A1.3

This Activity is the third of a series of three which together may provide the basis of appropriate evidence for your S/NVQ portfolio. The others are Activities 4 and 6. If you are intending to take this course of action, it might be better to write your answers on separate sheets of paper.

In Activity 6 we asked you to define your own job in terms of inputs, processes and outputs. Now we want you to consider, first of all, how your job's processes are (or should be) monitored and measured For instance 'Process X should take no longer than 2 hours; the start and finish time is automatically recorded by the computer software used; weekly reports are reviewed by the departmental manager and exceptions are investigated'.

The second part of this activity is to take one or, at most, two processes and devise your own internal audit programme, in the style illustrated above.

Remember that an 'audit' is an investigation to determine whether a system's processes, checks and controls are working properly and the system is doing what it is supposed to do. Your audit programme should include specific tests in the form of questions (the first part of this activity should help you to formulate these) and it should suggest how the test can be carried out.

Finally, using your internal audit programme, conduct an internal audit of the process or processes you chose.

Monitoring and measurement of product (8.2.4)

Even if the organization has decided to ignore or exclude the detailed **product** monitoring and measurement requirements under Section 7.6 because they are inappropriate, it is still required to make some effort to verify that product characteristics are being met, and it should keep a record of product monitoring and measuring activities.

For instance the virtue and appeal of a hand-made pottery vase might be precisely that it does not use any of the sophisticated modern methods of manufacture. But even though each vase is unique, that does not mean that it need not be monitored to make sure it is fit for its purpose. If it is meant to hold water then it should be tested to make sure that it does not leak before it is sold.

8.3 Control of nonconforming products

A nonconforming product is any product that your organization produces that does not conform to the customer's expectations for some reason: it is the wrong size or shape; it is delivered late; it breaks the first time it is used, and so on.

To meet this standard you will need to:

- take measures to **prevent the delivery** of nonconforming products. Ideally this means developing a quality management system that is so good that nonconforming products can never be delivered. Failing that, it means taking positive action to test products before sending them out;
- **eliminate or correct** product nonconformities. Records should be kept describing product nonconformities and the actions taken to deal with them.

If you do happen to deliver nonconforming products, your system should control subsequent events. In other words you should have an effective system for dealing with refunds, replacements or repairs, and with minimum fuss for the disappointed customer.

This requirement also says that the organization should decide how nonconforming products should be identified and how they should be handled. This sounds simpler than it is.

For instance, suppose your organization makes staplers. Is one of your staplers a nonconforming product if the customer uses it to stick up wallpaper and finds it is not very good for wallpaper hanging? Is the stapler a nonconforming product if the customer buys very cheap staples, not made by your organization, and finds that they buckle too easily before penetrating the paper? Probably no, in both cases, but the point is that such matters need to be thought about **before** you deliver the product.

8.4 Analysis of data

This requirement simply emphasizes the need to determine, collect and analyze the information needed to **evaluate and improve** the organization's quality system. Specifically, it mentions information about customers, suppliers, products and processes.

Note that it is not enough just to **collect** information. For instance, a computerized inventory system might automatically collect information, such as the date on which each order for supplies is placed and the date on which each order is fulfilled.

This is a good start, but quality system auditors will also be looking to see if this information is **analyzed** – perhaps in the form of league tables of suppliers, ranking them in order of speed of delivery – and **acted upon** – for instance by removing the slowest suppliers from the preferred suppliers list.

8.5 Improvement

Continuous improvement (8.5.1)

This requirement emphasizes, once again, that if an effective quality management system is in place there will always be room for improvement. Organizations should use the information from audits, management reviews, corrective and preventive actions and so on to generate improvements.

For instance, consider again the stapler company whose staplers were not suitable for wallpaper hanging and didn't work with some other organizations' staples.

Although this did not appear to be the stapler organization's problem, it is still potentially useful information. Why not produce a stapler that can be used for hanging wallpaper, if that is what customers want? Why not produce a stapler that can be adjusted to cope with varying qualities of staples?

This is what continuous improvement is all about.

Corrective action (8.5.2)

Of course, if your adjustable stapler **still** does not do what you now claim it can do, you need to take immediate action to put it right. This is what ISO 9001 has to say:

- review nonconformities and determine what causes them;
- evaluate whether corrective action is needed and if so take the appropriate action;
- record the results that your corrective actions achieve and examine the effectiveness of your corrective actions.

Preventive action (8.5.3)

Better, in the long run, than corrective action is action that spots potential nonconformities in advance and **prevents** them from occurring.

For instance, your new adjustable stapler may lead manufacturers of staples to produce even worse quality staples!

ISO 9001 says that your quality management system should anticipate things like this. Your adjustable stapler probably needs to be even more sensitive than you first thought.

- Detect potential nonconformities, identify their causes and study their effects
- Evaluate whether you need to take preventive action and if so develop preventive actions to eliminate the causes, and take them when necessary
- Record the results that your preventive actions achieve and examine the effectiveness of your preventive actions.

Self-assessment 2

15 mins

1 What is the difference between a product standard and a systems standard?

2 What are the four generic product categories, under ISO 9000?

3 Why might an organization decide that it needs to develop a quality management system?

4 What do you understand by the term 'control of documents' in a quality management system?

5 A quality policy should make a specific commitment, but to what?

6   Quality objectives should be SMART. What does SMART stand for?

7   What, in brief, does ISO 9001 say about human resources?

8   In what circumstances can Section 7 of ISO 9001 be ignored?

9   Who determines requirements related to an organization's products?

10   A product may never be realized if the release date is constantly put off to accommodate each and every new idea. How can this be avoided?

11   Give four examples of controls over production and service provision.

12   What is a 'special' process?

13   What are the requirements in Section 8 of ISO 9001 intended to ensure?

14   What is an internal audit?

15   How should an organization control nonconforming products?

Answers to these questions can be found on page 114.

9 Summary

- In the UK the **British Standards Institution (BSI)** is the primary standards-setting body and it has adopted standards produced by the Comité Européen de Normalisation (CEN) and the International Organization for Standardization (ISO).
- There are two types of standards: **product standards** set out requirements for particular types of product; **systems standards** set out requirements for the good organization and management of processes.
- The BS EN ISO 9000: 2000 family is made up of **four principal standards**: ISO 9000, ISO 9001, ISO 9004 and ISO 19011.
- **Key concepts** in the ISO 9000:2000 family are: customer focus; continuous improvement; top management leadership and involvement; and a process approach.
- **Certification** under ISO 9001 is desirable for many organizations. This is achieved following an audit by an independent Registrar.
- The main sections and subsections of **ISO 9001** are as follows.

4   Quality management system
   4.1   General requirements
   4.2   Documentation requirements

5   Management responsibility
   5.1   Management commitment
   5.2   Customer focus
   5.3   Quality policy
   5.4   Planning
   5.5   Responsibility, authority and communication
   5.6   Management review

6   Resource management
   6.1   Quality resources
   6.2   Human resources
   6.3   Infrastructure
   6.4   Work environment

7   Product realization
   7.1   Planning of product realization
   7.2   Customer-related processes
   7.3   Design and development
   7.4   Purchasing
   7.5   Production and service provision
   7.6   Control of monitoring and measuring devices

8   Measurement, analysis and improvement
   8.1   General
   8.2   Monitoring and measurement
   8.3   Control of nonconforming products
   8.4   Analysis of data
   8.5   Improvement

Session C
Quality control and statistics

1 Introduction

Quality means conformance to requirements, not goodness.[1]
Our focus of interest now turns to **process quality**, or **quality control**. The aim of quality control is to determine whether products conform to an agreed specification.

This session is a brief introduction to the statistics used in quality control, and what you learn in this session will be applied in Session D. Statistics is concerned with collecting, analysing, interpreting and presenting data. Statistics is important in quality control because quality control involves handling lots of data – mainly in the form of numbers.

One of the easiest things to do with a set of numbers is to work out the **average** (also called the 'mean'); that's what we'll look at first.

Then we'll go on to discuss ways of measuring the **variability or 'spread'** of a set of numbers. Two main techniques are used here: the **range** and the **standard deviation**.

EXTENSION 3
The book *Statistics* by Frank Owen and Ron Jones covers all the topics in statistics and probability that we will deal with in this workbook. You may want to go further into the subject by taking up this Extension.

[1] Philip B. Crosby *Quality is Still Free*, McGraw-Hill, 1995.

2 The mean, the range and the standard deviation

2.1 The mean

Imagine you are investigating the time spent on the telephone by your sales team. You arrange to have the calls timed over a period of a month, and collect a lot of data. You look at the figures for the first day and find that forty calls have been made. The time taken, in seconds, for the calls is as follows:

193	21	163	73	110	160	143	50	88	49
142	53	205	105	100	136	184	169	87	142
76	93	102	135	107	120	44	166	202	73
204	45	135	85	95	63	155	147	61	169

How can you work out the average length of time for these calls?

The first thing to do is to total all the figures. Then, knowing the total, you can divide by the number of calls to calculate the average.

The total of all the calls = 4650

The number of calls = 40

So the average, or mean, of this data $= \dfrac{4650}{40} =$ 116.25 seconds

The mean or average of a set of values is the total of all the values divided by the number of values in the set.

The mean is sometimes indicated by the symbol $\bar{x}$ (pronounced 'x bar').

2.2 The range

Suppose a first line manager in a factory making chinaware is checking the size of plates which have a theoretical size of 250 millimetres. He might pick out ten samples and get the following measurements (in millimetres):

Sample no.	1	2	3	4	5	6	7	8	9	10
Size (mm)	254	244	253	252	240	250	246	264	247	254

Our manager can first total these up and work out the mean.

The total is 2504. Therefore the mean $= \dfrac{2504}{10} = 250.4$ mm.

This is useful, as it would give an indication as to whether the average size is within tolerance. However, the manager would also like to have some measure of the variability of the plate size: **by how much** do sizes vary? After all, customers won't expect too much variation. One simple measure of variability, or spread of data, is **range**.

The range of a set of values is the largest value minus the smallest.

Activity 21

3 mins

Here is the list of plate sizes again:

Sample no.	1	2	3	4	5	6	7	8	9	10
Size (mm)	254	244	253	252	240	250	246	264	247	254

In this list, which is the largest?

_____

Which is the smallest?

_____

What is the range for this set of values?

_____

The largest size is sample 8 (264) and the smallest is sample 5 (240).

The range is the difference between the largest and the smallest:

$264 - 240 = 24$.

This is very useful, because although the mean size of the plates seems to be near to the nominal size of 250 millimetres, the range indicates that there is in fact a lot of variation in size.

The range is a helpful indication of spread, but, as we will see, it has its limitations.

2.3 The standard deviation

Standard deviation is one of the most commonly used tools in quality control. It is easier to grasp than you might think if you are not used to dealing with figures.

Activity 22

3 mins

Look at the following set of figures:

101, 102, 99, 101, 3, 100, 102, 102, 99, 101.

What is the range?

_____

Explain briefly why a measurement of range is not very useful in this context.

_____

_____

The range of the set of figures given is:

102 − 3 = 99.

However, if we ignore the lowest figure (3) the range becomes:

102 − 99 = 3.

So all the figures are in the range 102 − 99 except for one item which is a long way outside this range.

This example shows the main disadvantage of using the range as a measure of variation: odd single figures can distort the result.

A manager of a supermarket was interested in finding out how long customers had to wait in the checkout queues. After measuring times over several days, she found that a customer might expect to wait anything from zero to twelve minutes. However, when she examined the data, she found that only on two occasions out of about 15,000 was the wait as long as twelve minutes; otherwise, it never exceeded eight-and-a-half minutes.

A better method of measuring the spread or variability of data is needed. The one most often employed in quality control is called the **standard deviation**. The standard deviation largely overcomes the disadvantage of being distorted by unusual values that occur only very rarely.

Working out the standard deviation by hand takes a little more time than working out the range. On a scientific calculator it can be done automatically, simply by keying in each item of data and pressing a key to give the standard deviation function.

If you have access to a computer, standard deviations can be calculated using spreadsheet software as well as on more specialized packages.

> To work out the standard deviation on a calculator, you will need one with a square root $\sqrt{}$ function. The square root is a number or quantity that, when multiplied by itself, results in a given number or quantity. So the square root of 4 is 2, and the square root of 9 is 3, that is:
>
> $\sqrt{4}$ = 2 and
>
> $\sqrt{9}$ = 3.

Steps for calculating standard deviation

In case you don't have a scientific calculator or computer, the steps for working out the standard deviation by hand are set out below. There are six steps involved. Follow the steps and the example shown. You are not expected to remember the process.

Step	Example
	Data: The lengths of five cut pieces of cloth in centimetres: 123, 128, 113, 127, 125
1 Work out the mean of the set of values.	Total = 616 Mean = $\dfrac{616}{5}$ = 123.2
2 Subtract the mean from each value, to give the 'differences'. (If the mean is greater than the value, the difference will be negative.)	123 − 123.2 = −0.2 128 − 123.2 = 4.8 113 − 123.2 = −10.2 127 − 123.2 = 3.8 125 − 123.2 = 1.8
3 Take each of these differences and square it; that is, multiply it by itself. (Note that the answers are always positive, even if the differences are negative. A minus times a minus is a plus.)	−0.2 × −0.2 = 0.04 4.8 × 4.8 = 23.04 −10.2 × −10.2 = 104.04 3.8 × 3.8 = 14.44 1.8 × 1.8 = 3.24
4 Add up these squares.	0.04 + 23.04 + 104.04 + 14.44 + 3.24 = 144.8
5 Divide this sum by the number of items. The result is called the 'variance'.	$\dfrac{144.8}{5}$ = 28.96
6 Take the square root of the variance; this gives the standard deviation.	$\sigma = \sqrt{28.96} = 5.38\,\text{cm}$ (approx.)

So the standard deviation for this example is approximately 5.38 centimetres. This is quite a small figure in relation to the mean, which indicates that the spread or variability of the data is within fairly narrow limits. In other words, the data are tightly clustered, rather than being widely scattered.

The standard deviation is usually denoted by the Greek character σ (pronounced sigma).

3 The distribution of data

So far, we have learned how to work out the mean, the range, and the standard deviation. So, if we have some quality control data, we can find their average value, and measure their spread.

Here's another set of numbers. These are the transit times (in minutes) of lorry-loads of materials travelling between two branches of a company, during one week.

32	27	28	26	31	29	26	31	23	27	26	28	22	23
25	25	30	21	27	26	27	25	24	29	22	20	23	28
28	26	24	24	33	19	25	27	26	25	29	22	27	25
30	29	21	26	24	25	24	28	23	27	25	30	27	28
26	26	24											

The quality manager looks at this data and works out the total, the mean and the range.

Activity 24 ·

3 mins

What is the mean and the range of the above data? (To save you adding up the figures, the total is 1534.)

_____

_____

The total = 1534 and the number of values = 59.

So the mean – $\dfrac{1534}{59}$ = 26.

The lowest and highest numbers are 19 and 33, so the range is 33 – 19 = 14.

Next, the manager would like to know how frequently each number occurs. The easiest way to do this is to tick them off on a tally chart. He writes down all the possible numbers in the range, then goes through the list, ticking off each number one by one:

Frequency

19	/	1
20	/	1
21	//	2
22	///	3
23	////	4
24	///// /	6
25	##### ///	8
26	##### ////	9
27	##### ///	8
28	##### /	6
29	////	4
30	///	3
31	//	2
32	/	1
33	/	1

Now the manager can plot these numbers on a **graph**. He draws two lines (called **axes**) perpendicular to one another. On the horizontal axis he marks off a scale showing the times, from one end of the range to the other. On the vertical axis he marks off another scale showing the frequency that each time occurs:

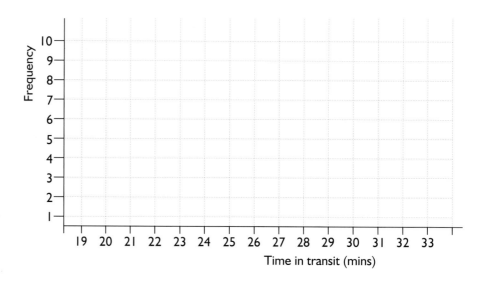

Now our quality manager puts a cross for each value on the horizontal axis, at the point on the vertical axis which corresponds to its frequency. He then joins up the crosses.

The next figure shows what the graph looks like:

This is a frequency distribution graph for the time-in-transit data in our example.

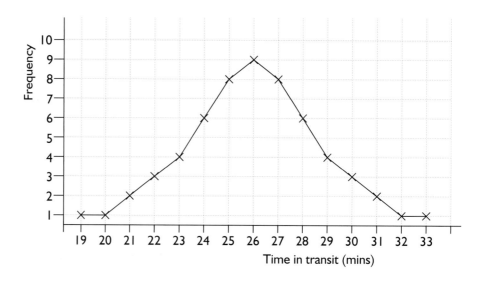

The shape of this graph reflects the following facts:

■ the curve peaks at 26 minutes, which is also the mean;
■ other values occur less frequently, the further away they are from this central value;
■ there is a distinct 'bell shape' to the graph.

Of course, the values in this example were carefully chosen so that it would turn out like this. However, it was designed to illustrate some interesting ideas.

If we draw a smooth curve, instead of joining the points with straight lines, we get the general shape shown in the next figure:

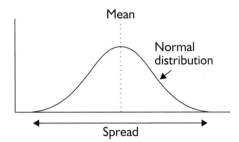

This is the general shape of the normal distribution.

This is called the **normal distribution**. It is symmetric about its mean. It is bell shaped and the 'fatness' or spread of the bell is measured by the standard deviation of the data. If σ is large, the spread is wide, and if σ is small, the spread is narrow.

The normal distribution is a very special curve, because of the following remarkable fact.

If we take any large population of things or people, and measure some characteristic, the distribution of the data will be normal.

For example, all of these will be normally distributed:

- the waist measurements of people in any large organization;
- the measured lengths of a large shipment of screws;
- the amount of money spent daily in a shop over a long period;
- the time taken to perform a certain task by individuals in a large group;
- the amount of jam in jam-jars of the same size;
- the number of spelling mistakes occurring per book, in all the books of a publisher;
- the lengths of the incisions made by a surgeon for a particular operation;
- the heights of daffodils on a day in spring;
- the winning numbers in the national lottery over a long period of time.

There are so many possible examples, it would not be difficult to continue this list until we had filled the whole workbook. (And then we could find a normal distribution governing the number of letters per word, and the number of words per page!)

Large populations of all kinds, where there is a tendency to cluster round a mean, display a normal distribution. Going back to our quality manager and his transit times, we noted that the data was approximately normal. Now we can say that, if he were to take a large enough number of samples, the distribution of the data would indeed be normal.

3.1 Varying the mean

As you can see in the diagram, the mean is in the centre of the curve. The spread can be measured by the standard deviation. What happens to the curve if the mean is different?

Activity 25

4 mins

The general shape of the normal distribution is shown again on the right.

Suppose there are three sets of data, all of which have a distribution the shape of a normal curve, and the same standard deviation, but each has a different mean:

Set A has a mean of 10

Set B has a mean of 20 and

Set C has a mean of 30.

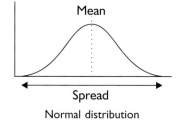

Mean

Spread

Normal distribution

On the axes below, sketch the normal curves for these three sets.

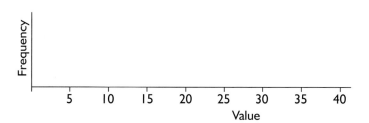

Frequency

5   10   15   20   25   30   35   40

Value

The answer to this activity can be found on page 117.

3.2 Varying the spread

As we've discussed, the standard deviation is a measure of the spread of data. Therefore if one set of data are clustered closely around the mean, they would have a smaller standard deviation than a set of data which vary a long way from the mean.

Activity 26

3 mins

That being so, what would you expect to happen to the shape of the normal curve as the standard deviation gets bigger? Would it

Get taller and narrower? ☐

Get shorter and wider? ☐

Stay the same? ☐

The answer is that the curve gets shorter and wider as the standard deviation increases. This is what we might expect, because there is a greater 'spread' of data and there aren't so many items of data at the centre.

The next diagram shows three different normal curves, each with the same mean but with different standard deviations.

These distribution curves are based on data with the same mean, but different amounts of 'spread'.

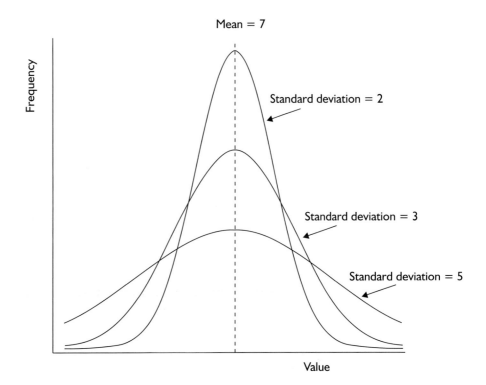

In the next diagram, the mean is 20, and the standard deviation is 4. Six vertical lines are drawn showing:

■ the mean, plus one standard deviation, marked $+1\sigma$;
■ the mean, minus one standard deviation marked -1σ;
■ the mean, plus two standard deviations marked $+2\sigma$;
■ the mean, minus two standard deviations -2σ;
■ the mean, plus three standard deviations $+3\sigma$;
■ the mean, minus three standard deviations -3σ.

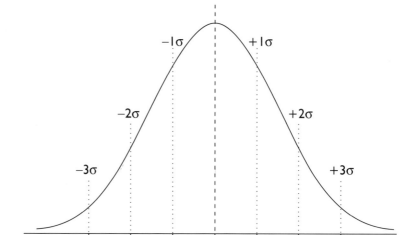

This is a normal distribution curve of a set of data that have a mean of 20, and a standard deviation of 4 ($\sigma = 4$).

The standard deviation is 4, so 'mean $+1\sigma$' is $20 + 4 = 24$. Similarly, you can see that the mean minus two standard deviations is 'mean -2σ' = $20 - 2 \times 4 = 12$.

Once we get to three standard deviations either side of the mean, nearly the whole of the curve is covered. So almost all of the data lies between the lines '-3σ' and '$+3\sigma$'.

The interesting thing is that this doesn't just apply to one particular normal curve – it applies to **all** normal curves.

This means that

once we have worked out the standard deviation for any kind of data which displays the normal curve, we know that nearly all of the data lies between three standard deviations either side of the mean.

To be a little more specific than this, in any normal distribution:

■ 68.26 per cent of the data will lie between one standard deviation either side of the mean;

- 95.44 per cent of the data will lie between two standard deviations either side of the mean;
- 99.72 per cent of the data will lie between three standard deviations either side of the mean.

You can see how these add up in the next figure.

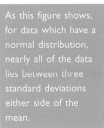

As this figure shows, for data which have a normal distribution, nearly all of the data lies between three standard deviations either side of the mean.

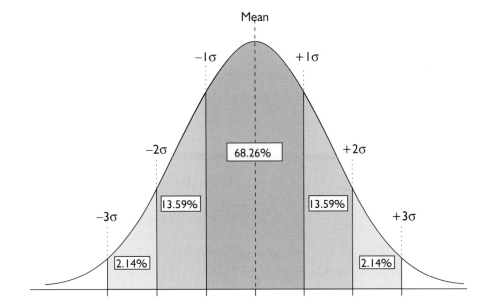

Activity 27 · 3 mins

Looking at the above diagram, what percentage of the data will lie between plus and minus two standard deviations?

I hope you agree that a total of **95.44** per cent of the data will lie between plus and minus two standard deviations.

Now try the question in the next activity.

Activity 28 · 3 mins

Some data are distributed normally, and have a mean of 50 and a standard deviation of 8. Between what values of data will 99.72 per cent of the data lie?

We know that 99.72 per cent of the data will lie between three standard deviations either side of the mean, and that one standard deviation is 8. Therefore:

three standard deviations = $3 \times 8 = 24$.

So 99.7 per cent of the data will lie between:

$50 + 24 = 74$ and

$50 - 24 = 26$.

This is the main point to remember:

99.72 per cent of the data in any normal distribution will lie between three standard deviations either side of the mean.

Self-assessment 3 · 20 mins

1   Find the mean and the range of the following data, taken from a manager's record of the weekly overtime worked by his team:

32	9	72	33	56	18	7	98	93	35
33	8	10	81	69	84	10	13	59	80

2 Calculate the standard deviation of the following data set. If you are able to work out the answer on a scientific calculator, use that instead of following the steps listed.

Step	Your calculation
	Data: the typing speed of five typists in words per minute: 80, 57, 72, 48, 63
1 Work out the mean of the set of values.	
2 Subtract the mean from each value, to give the 'differences'.	
3 Take each of these differences and square it: multiply it by itself.	
4 Add up these squares.	
5 Divide this sum by the number of items. The result is called the 'variance'.	
6 Take the square root of the variance; this gives the standard deviation.	

3   A set of data, which are distributed normally, have a mean of 13 and a standard deviation of 2. Sketch a curve of this distribution on the axes below. Indicate the mean, and mark the position of each of $\bar{x} + 1\sigma$, $\bar{x} + 2\sigma$, $\bar{x} + 3\sigma$, $\bar{x} - 1\sigma$, $\bar{x} - 2\sigma$ and $\bar{x} - 3\sigma$.

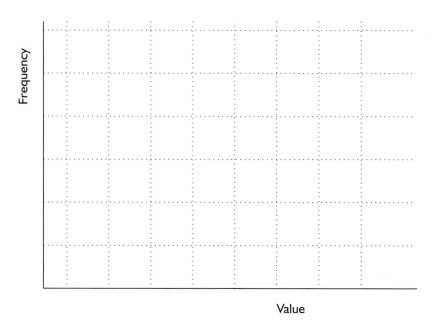

Value

4   Look at the next diagram, which is the normal distribution for a certain set of data. Between which points (from A, B, C, D, E, F, G) will the following percentages of the data lie?

a   68.26 per cent
b   81.85 per cent (there are two possible answers)
c   83.99 per cent (there are two possible answers)

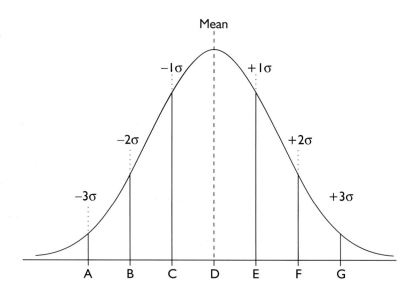

Answers to these questions can be found on pages 115–6.

4 Summary

■ The **mean** or **average** of a set of values is the total of all the values divided by the number of values in the set. It can be called $\bar{x}$ (pronounced 'x bar').

■ The **range** of a set of values is the largest value minus the smallest.

■ **Graphs** are ways of presenting information in the form of a diagram. A graph illustrates the connection between two sets of data.

■ The method of defining the spread or variability of data most often employed in quality control is called the **standard deviation**. Compared with the range, the standard deviation largely overcomes the disadvantage of being distorted by unusual values which occur only very rarely.

■ Data of all kinds is **normally distributed**. If we take any large population of things or people, and measure some characteristic, the distribution of the data will be normal.

■ Once we have worked out the standard deviation for any kind of data which displays the normal curve, we know that **99.72 per cent of the data in any normal distribution** will lie between three standard deviations either side of the mean.

Session D
Statistical process control

1 Introduction

Now that we've covered some basic statistics, we will start to apply it to quality problems.

First we look at one of the most important techniques in quality control: **sampling**. Sampling means picking out items at random from a large quantity. It is a technique applied whenever it is impractical to check everything, and it is useful in all kinds of work situations. To understand sampling, we need a little probability theory.

We then work through an example of how a **sampling plan** can be selected to ensure a certain **acceptable quality level** (AQL).

Next we move to the problem of ensuring that a work process stays within **tolerance limits**.

2 Sampling

To ensure conformity to an agreed standard, the quality of a product or a component must be inspected or measured.

However, it is impractical to check every item produced or purchased. For one thing, this would be too time-consuming and expensive.

The idea of sampling is that only some of the items are checked. Provided certain defined rules are followed

the proportion of defects in the sample should give an indication of the proportion of defects in the whole quantity.

Sampling is applied not only in all kinds of industry but in other areas of life:

A **random sample** is a sample chosen in such a way that every sample of the same size has the same chance of being selected.

- When financial auditors check the books of a company, they rarely verify all the invoices and other documents. Instead, they select a certain percentage of them. If errors are found in these samples, the auditors will usually check further. Auditing can be called financial quality control.
- To find out what members of the public think about a certain subject (the outcome of an election), a 'poll' may be undertaken. Here, a random selection of people are asked their opinions. Provided the sample is large enough, and is truly random, the result will be a fairly good indication of the opinions of the public as a whole.
- When a swimming pool supervisor wants to check that the water has the right chemical balance, does not contain too many bacteria, etc., she does not check all the water in the pool, but merely takes a very small sample. In this case, if the water is thoroughly mixed, she can safely assume that the sample is representative of the condition of the rest.
- Many kinds of goods can't be tested without destroying them. For example, to find out how long an electric light bulb will last, the only thing to do is to run it until it fails. So, if you want to work out the average life of bulbs on a production line in a certain period, you can't leave them all on until they fail. But you can run a small random sample of them, and the results will give you a good indication of the average life of the whole batch.

Perhaps you can think of other examples where sampling is used.

3 Acceptable quality level (AQL)

Imagine you are in charge of inspecting goods coming into a factory, or a department store.

Activity 29 · 2 mins

If you choose to sample the goods, can you guarantee to find all defects?

YES   NO

If 100 per cent checking is used, can you guarantee to find all defects?

YES   NO

EXTENSION 4
If you'd like to study the subject of AQL and other aspects of quality control in greater depth, *A Practical Approach To Quality Control* by R.H. Caplen is a good source of information.

As we have already discussed, no amount of sampling will **guarantee** that all defects are found; neither will checking every item.

Nevertheless, organizations have to control quality, and that often means sampling, because checking every item just isn't feasible. In practice, organizations checking goods have to ask the question:

'What percentage of defects can we tolerate at this point in the operation?'

This may seem a strange question in view of our discussions in the first two sessions of this workbook. However, it is a realistic one. The whole purpose of quality control is to find out the level of quality being reached, so that it can be improved if necessary.

Acceptable quality level (AQL) is the maximum percentage of defects in a sample that can be considered acceptable as a process average.

To decide this, the aim of any organization concerned with quality is of course to have **zero** defects, and the term 'acceptable quality level' should not be misunderstood. The question is never: 'How many mistakes are we allowed to make?', because AQL is not intended as a way of letting organizations relax their standards. AQL is only designed to answer the question: 'How well are we doing at this stage?'

The term 'Acceptable quality level (AQL)' does not mean that it is acceptable to make mistakes or to lower your standards.

Once the AQL is decided upon, the next question is:

'What size sample must we take in order to have a high probability of achieving the AQL?'

Although it is possible to calculate this for any particular size of batch and AQL, using the laws of probability, there are tools to make it easier.

■ Modern production software is likely to have facilities that calculate the appropriate sample size for you.

■ There are some (free) Internet-based applications that do the calculations for you.

■ A number of publishers produce sets of sampling inspection tables, covering a very wide variety of situations. One of the best-known is the International Organization for Standardization's ISO 2859 series. (The British Standard equivalent, which is identical, is the BS 6000 series.)

Let's take an example and use a sampling inspection table from ISO 2859–1 to decide firstly what size sample is needed; secondly, how to calculate the AQL.

Items of kitchen equipment are purchased by a mail-order company which intends to re-sell them to its customers. Naturally the company wants to be fairly certain that the items meet the required specification, so it arranges for each incoming batch to be sampled.

Let's assume in our example that the parts are purchased in batches of 600. Let's also assume that the inspection team is working to an AQL of 1 per cent. This means that if a defect rate of more than one item in 100 – or six in 600 – is found, the batch will be rejected. The question is 'how big should the sample be?'

An illustration of an ISO 2859–1 sampling inspection table is shown below. (We cannot show you a whole table because there is not room, and it will be simpler if we focus on a small part.)

The table is a bit mind-boggling at first, especially when you see a whole one.
So how do we read this table?

Batch size code letter	Sample size	Acceptance quality limit, AQL, in percent non-conforming items and noncomformities per 100 items (normal inspection)											
		0.040	0.065	0.10	0.15	0.25	0.4	0.65	1.0	1.5	2.5	4	6.5
		Ac Re	Ac Re	Ac Re	Ac Re	Ac Re	Ac Re	Ac Re	Ac Re	Ac Re	Ac Re	Ac Re	Ac Re
J	80					0 1			1 2	2 3	3 4	5 6	7 8	10 11
K	125				0 1			1 2	2 3	3 4	5 6	7 8	10 11	14 15
L	200		0 1			1 2	2 3	3 4	5 6	7 8	10 11	14 15	21 22	
M	315	0 1			1 2	2 3	3 4	5 6	7 8	10 11	14 15	21 22		
N	500			1 2	2 3	3 4	5 6	7 8	10 11	14 15	21 22			

■ **Step 1**

We need to know first which **batch size code letter** we should use. (These are listed in the column on the far left-hand side.) To do this, we need to refer to another table (see below).

Although the tables cover an enormous number of possible circumstances, in most circumstances you should use **level II**.

Lot size		General inspection levels		
From	**To**	I	II	III
281	500	F	H	J
501	1200	G	J	K
1201	3200	H	K	L
3201	10000	J	L	M
10001	35000	K	M	N
35001	150000	L	N	P
15001	500000	M	P	Q
500001	and over	N	Q	R

In our example we have a **batch size** of 600. Under 'Lot size', this falls between 501 and 1200. The letter in column II of 'General inspection levels' is J.

■ **Step 2**

Here is the table again. We now know we will be using **row J** and that indicates that our **sample size** (see second column) should be 80.

■ **Step 3**

In our example we are told that we are working to an AQL of 1%. So we look

Batch size code letter	Sample size	Acceptance quality limit, AQL, in percent non-conforming items and noncomformities per 100 items (normal inspection)											
		0.040	0.065	0.10	0.15	0.25	0.4	0.65	1.0	1.5	2.5	4	6.5
		Ac Re	Ac Re	Ac Re	Ac Re	Ac Re	Ac Re	Ac Re	Ac Re	Ac Re	Ac Re	Ac Re	Ac Re
F	20							0 1			1 2	2 3	3 4
G	32						0 1			1 2	2 3	3 4	5 6
H	50					0 1			1 2	2 3	3 4	5 6	7 8
J	80				0 1			1 2	2 3	3 4	5 6	7 8	10 11
K	125			0 1			1 2	2 3	3 4	5 6	7 8	10 11	14 15
L	200		0 1			1 2	2 3	3 4	5 6	7 8	10 11	14 15	21 22
M	315	0 1			1 2	2 3	3 4	5 6	7 8	10 11	14 15	21 22	
N	500			1 2	2 3	3 4	5 6	7 8	10 11	14 15	21 22		

along the top line until we reach the column headed 1.0. Beneath this figure are two abbreviations, 'Ac' and 'Re'.

Ac is the 'acceptance number', i.e. the **maximum number of defects** allowed in a sample of 80 for a batch of 600 to pass inspection. In this case Ac = 2.

Re is the 'rejection number' and it = 3. If **3 or more defects** are found in a sample, then the batch has failed the test.

■ **Conclusion**

A sample of 80 items from each batch should be tested. If there are **no more than two** defects the batch passes the test, but if **three or more** are found the batch should be rejected.

You will notice that part of row J seems to consist of arrows. (In fact if you were to look at the full table almost all of it would show arrows.) What does this mean?

An arrow, for example in the 0.040%, 0.065% and 0.10% columns, indicates that there is not a **valid sampling plan** for a given combination of AQL and sample size. If we were using letter K and sampling at 0.065% the table directs to move **down** to row L; if we were using letter N and sampling at 0.040% the table directs us to move **up** to row M.

Activity 30

3 mins

Using the tables from the example above, suppose we are working to an AQL of 0.25 per cent and have a batch size of 1500.

■ How many samples should be taken from each batch? _____

■ What is the maximum number of defects allowed in the sample for the batch to be passed? _____

■ What number of defects (as a minimum) found in the sample would result in the batch being rejected? _____

See how your answers compare with the following. If you got different answers, make sure you picked the right letter (we gave you no reason not to test at Level II) and followed the arrows properly.

- A sample of 200 should be checked in each batch (the arrow directs you to the nearest available equivalent i.e. batch size < = 200).
- If no defects are found, the batch should be accepted.
- If one or more defects are found, the batch should be rejected.

If this sampling plan is followed there is a high probability that the number of defectives will not exceed the required AQL. Over the longer term, sampling plans like this can be relied upon.

4 Control limits

Now let's consider another kind of problem in quality control: how to monitor the production of an item so that it continues to be made to specification.

For our example this time, assume that a lathe is being used to make spindles.

The spindles must be manufactured to fairly close dimensions or they won't fit properly in a bearing. However, it would be impossible to make them all precisely the same size – there's bound to be some variation. The designer of the component would set a **tolerance** on the dimensions: the specification would give the dimensions and state that they should be made to these dimensions **plus** or **minus** (±) some amount.

As an example, let's say that the spindle has a nominal diameter of 52 mm. The tolerance is 51.95 to 52.05 mm; another way of saying it is that the spindles should be 52.00 mm ± 0.05 mm.

If the process has just been set up, we may not know for sure whether it is capable of making the spindles within tolerance, so we would need to make this assessment.

Once it has been working well for some time, the process may then drift out of adjustment. The aim of the inspection team would be to try to prevent incorrectly sized spindles being produced. This means detecting when the process is drifting out of adjustment so that it can be corrected **before** it starts producing spindles that are out of tolerance.

Activity 31

2 mins

Imagine you are the line manager responsible for making sure the spindles are inspected and within tolerance. Assuming that it would be too time-consuming and expensive to check every item, what alternative approach to this problem could you take?

_____

_____

As we've already agreed, if it isn't practical to check every item, it seems sensible to **sample**. As manager, you would no doubt instruct your team to take samples of the output of the lathe and check for the spindles diameter size.

Let's imagine that you have suggested that the team take five spindles every hour and measure them. They average each set of five measurements and get the following results:

Sample means (the mean of each sample of five spindles)				
52.01	52.00	52.02	51.99	51.96
51.97	51.96	51.98	51.97	51.96

Activity 32

3 mins

What is the mean of these figures?

_____

The mean of these sample means $= \dfrac{519.82}{10} = 51.98$ approximately.

How should the results be recorded? We could draw a graph. By plotting the sample means, we would get a graph something like this:

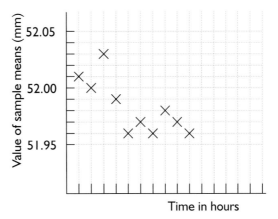

This is a graph of the average of each hourly set of five samples, measured for spindle diameter.

But we can improve on this diagram. The aim is to produce spindles of 52.00 mm diameter. Also, there is a specified tolerance, so we know that the highest acceptable figure for the diameter is 52.05 mm, and the lowest 51.95 mm. It seems a good idea, then, to draw in lines on the graph for the target diameter, and for the tolerance limits. You can see the result below.

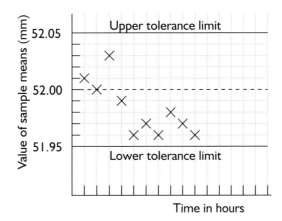

The tolerance limits provide a visual indication as to whether a process is out of tolerance.

Activity 33

2 mins

By glancing at the chart above, would you say:

■ all the samples are within the tolerance limits?   YES   NO

■ there is any drift in one direction or another?   YES   NO

By adding lines for the tolerance limits, I hope you agree that all the samples are within the tolerance limits. It isn't perhaps so easy to detect evidence of drift, but we can see that at the start the readings are near or above the centre line, and later are mainly nearer the lower limit.

4.1 Process capability

The next step is to determine whether the machine is capable of producing spindles within the desired tolerance for a sustained period. This is called the **process capability**. (Although the process has produced some spindles within tolerance, we cannot be sure that this was not pure chance.)

In general, a process is said to be capable if the mean of its sample means, plus and minus three standard deviations, is within the process tolerance limits.

First, we work out the mean and the standard deviation.

Activity 34 · 3 mins

What can we tell about the data by knowing the standard deviation?

_____

_____

One thing we know from our earlier discussions is that we can expect 99.72 per cent of the readings **from any process** to fall within three standard deviations either side of the mean of that process.

The standard deviation of these sample means is 0.021. We already worked out the mean of the sample means as 51.98.

Using these figures:

mean = 51.98 mm; σ = 0.021 mm

So mean plus three standard deviations = mean + (3 $\times$ σ)

= 51.98 + (3 $\times$ 0.021) = 52.043 mm

And mean minus three standard deviations = mean − (3 × σ)

$$= 51.98 − (3 × 0.021) = 51.92 \text{ mm.}$$

This is interesting. The figure of 51.92 is **outside our tolerance limit**. What it tells us is that, even though so far we may have found no samples outside the tolerance band, we can expect that some spindles **will** fall outside this band.

This is the normal distribution superimposed on the tolerance limit chart. (The shaded area shows the part of the distribution outside the tolerance limits.)

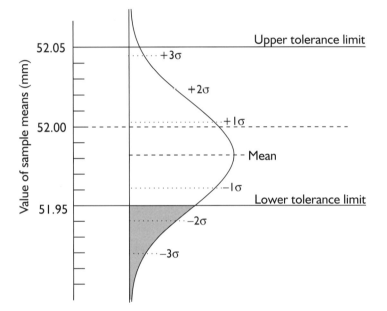

This is easier to see in the diagram. The normal distribution curve is turned on its side, so that the tolerance band and the spread of the process data are both on the same axis. You can see how the normal curve for the data collected (or rather, that part of the normal curve that is plus and minus three standard deviations from the mean) **overlaps** one of the tolerance limits.

It seems therefore that our process is **not** at present capable. Once the mean and standard deviation are calculated, the spread of the data is greater than the spread of the tolerance band. It follows that we would need to make some change to the process to make it capable of producing spindles consistently within tolerance.

Activity 35 ·

3 mins

Look again at the last diagram. If the data is to be in tolerance, most of the normal distribution curve must be inside the tolerance limits.

How would the data need to be different in order for its normal distribution curve (i.e. three standard deviations either side of the mean) to fit inside the tolerance limits? Pick the correct answer or answers, and then briefly explain your choice.

a The mean of the data would have to be nearer 52.00 mm, with the same spread ☐

b The data would have to be less widely spread, but with the same mean. ☐

c The mean would have to be nearer 52.00 mm **and** the data would have to be less widely spread. ☐

_____

_____

_____

_____

_____

a Looking at the diagram, let's think first what would happen if the mean of the data were nearer 52.00 mm, but with the data being just as widely spread. If the normal curve were moved upwards, the portion that is plus and minus three standard deviations from the mean still would **not** fit inside the tolerance limits, would it?

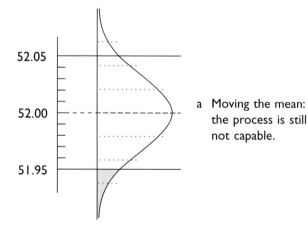

a Moving the mean: the process is still not capable.

b By making the spread of data (and therefore the shape of the normal curve) **a lot** narrower, but **without** changing the mean, the portion that is plus and minus three standard deviations from the mean **could** be made to fit inside the limits.

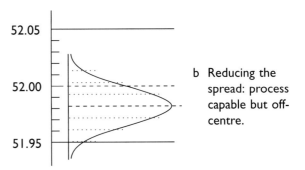

b Reducing the spread: process capable but off-centre.

c If the spread was **slightly** narrower, **and** the mean was nearer 52.00 mm, again it **could** be made to fit inside the tolerance limits.

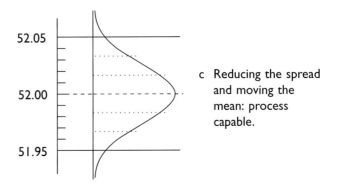

c Reducing the spread and moving the mean: process capable.

So answers b and c are in fact both correct. It's simply a decision of whether 99.72 per cent of the normal distribution will fit inside the 'window' of the tolerance limits.

We can summarize by repeating the point made earlier:

In general, a process is said to be capable if the mean of its sample means, plus and minus three standard deviations, is within the process tolerance limits.

There is a general formula for process capability, assuming there is an upper and lower tolerance limit. It is:

$$\text{process capability } (C_p) = \frac{\text{total specification tolerance}}{\text{total effective range}}$$

Here, C_p is an index of process capability. If C_p is less than one, the process is **not** capable. If C_p is greater than one, the process **is** capable. The greater the value of C_p above one, the greater the capability.

The **total specification tolerance** is the 'intended range' or 'design range'.

The **total effective range** is the 'actual range' = six standard deviations.

So that:

$$C_p = \frac{T_U - T_L}{6\sigma}$$

where T_U and T_L are the upper and lower specification limits, and σ is the standard deviation for the data.

This follows from what we have already discussed. It is important, of course, that the data is centred.

The following diagram illustrates three possible situations.

a The process is capable.
b The process is not capable.
c The process would be capable if it were centred.

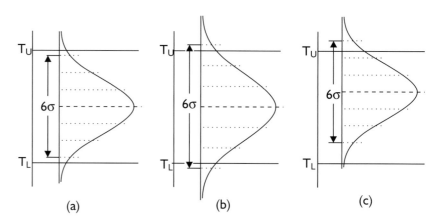

(a) (b) (c)

Activity 36

3 mins

Thinking now about the actual work process, what possible reasons might there be for a process not to be capable?

_____

_____

_____

There could be lots of possible reasons. Often, it is the first line manager who has to make the decision about what is causing the problem, and to try to put it right.

The temptation is to ignore what the statistics are telling you. There is usually a lot of pressure on keeping a process going in spite of problems. Managers have even been known to alter the results and pretend the process is still within tolerance, because they know that is the easier course of action.

But work processes go out of tolerance for a variety of reasons, many of them easily rectified. For instance it may be that:

- the lighting is poor;
- a member of staff is inexperienced or needs further training;
- equipment requires adjustment;
- a part on a machine is worn and needs replacing;
- work material is defective;
- there is a problem with the design;
- closer monitoring of results is needed.

Activity 37

6 mins

Every September, a typical college might process around 15 000 enrolment forms, entering the data into computers. Inevitably errors are made, and these have to be found and corrected.

In one particular college, the managers aimed to reduce the overall error rate as much as possible through a series of measures (extra training, improvement of working conditions, and so on). It set a new initial target of ten errors per person per day.

Once the extra measures had been taken, and the 'process' had settled down, the daily error rate was recorded. The work of five people a day were checked thoroughly as a sample, and the following results were found:

Sample means of number of errors per day (the mean of each sample of five people)				
8	11	9	4	2
7	13	8	2	6

a Work out the mean of sample means and the standard deviation.

b Decide whether this work process is capable. (Hint: there is no 'lower tolerance limit'.)

_____

_____

_____

_____

_____

_____

_____

_____

The answer to this activity can be found on page 118.

4.2 Setting control limits

Assessing process capability is a useful way of determining whether the process is likely to produce output which is consistently within tolerance.

However, once the process has been set up, and is working normally, it may still drift out of tolerance at some point. It would be useful to have an early warning of this, and the procedure below is one way of monitoring the situation.

In the feedback to Activity 34 we looked at data from spindles produced by a lathe. Here are some different sample readings from the same lathe. Again, these are 'sample means' – the team has taken five samples at a time, averaged the result and then plotted the point.

Sample means (the mean of each set of five samples)					
52.03	52.01	52.02	52.03	52.02	52.03
52.03	52.02	52.03	52.01	52.02	52.02
52.01	52.00	51.99	51.98	51.98	51.98
51.99	51.98	51.98	51.97	51.96	51.96

This time the sample ranges are also calculated – that is, the difference between the highest and the lowest value in the sample – for each set of five samples. These are:

Sample range (the range of each set of five samples)					
0.013	0.010	0.010	0.004	0.003	0.022
0.022	0.021	0.021	0.032	0.023	0.003
0.016	0.012	0.023	0.013	0.018	0.042
0.020	0.005	0.012	0.002	0.020	0.011

Again, it's difficult to make sense of these figures until we plot them on a chart. First, the sample means are plotted, as before:

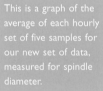

This is a graph of the average of each hourly set of five samples for our new set of data, measured for spindle diameter.

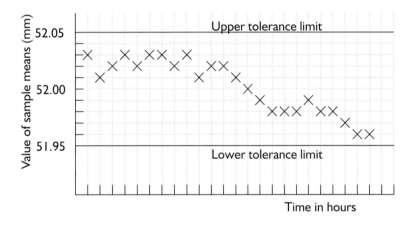

Here there seems to be definite evidence of a drift, even though again all the samples are within limits. This drift towards the lower end of the band suggests that the lathe may need readjustment.

(We could also plot the sample ranges but it wouldn't tell us very much at this stage. We will need to use them though, as you will see shortly.)

When should the operator be told to readjust the machine?

■ When the samples actually go outside the tolerance limit?

This may be too late. Every item outside tolerance is scrap. It is possible to pick good samples even when many defective items are being produced, so the delay may result in a lot of rework.

■ Well before the samples go outside the limit?

Yes – but when exactly?

One way to solve this problem is to set **control limits inside** the tolerance limits. If we did this we would get a warning that something was wrong before the tolerance limit was reached – which is our aim.

The only question now is **where** exactly to set the control limits.

In fact, the control limits are calculated by averaging the ranges of the samples.

The steps are as follows:

■ First of all we work out the mean range. This is the average of all the sample ranges.

As we discussed earlier, the range of a single sample will only give us a rough indication of its variability. However, the mean range gives a good indication of variability. In fact, there is an exact relation between the true mean range and the standard deviation.

In our example, the mean range works out to 0.01575.

■ Next we multiply this mean range by a constant, according to the sample size. This constant is given in the following table:[1]

Sample size	2	3	4	5	6	7	8
Constant	1.51	1.16	1.02	0.95	0.90	0.87	0.84

Our sample size was 5, so we use 0.95 as a constant. Thus we have:

$$0.01575 \times 0.95 = 0.015 \text{ (approx.)}$$

On the average chart, we draw the two control limits so that they are each this distance (Constant × Mean range) inside the tolerance limits.

The **upper control limit** works out to 52.05 − 0.015 = 52.035

The **lower control limit** works out to 51.95 + 0.015 = 51.965.

[1] Table quoted in R. H. Caplan, *A Practical Approach to Quality Control*, p. 340. See Extension 4 on page 112.

The new limits are then drawn in on the chart, as shown in the next figure. The idea is that when a control limit is breached, it is treated as an early indication that the corresponding tolerance limit may be exceeded.

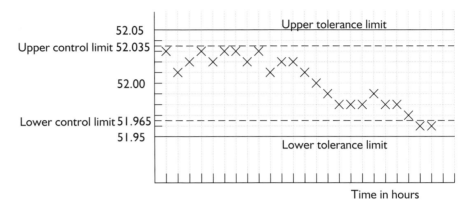

We have put control limits on our graph, calculated using the range of the data.

Time in hours

Activity 38 · 2 mins

Draw a ring around those samples in the chart above which are outside the control limits.

You should have ringed the last two sets of samples at the bottom right-hand corner of the chart. It is at this point that the lathe should be readjusted.

To summarize:

■ The problem is one that is frequently encountered in quality control: how to monitor work processes so as to:

■ make sure that they are capable of producing results that lie within agreed tolerance limits; and

■ detect when the process is drifting out of tolerance.

■ Sampling is used, and the sample means are plotted on a control chart. The tolerance limits are drawn on the chart.

■ Process capability (determined by whether the mean of its sample means, plus and minus three standard deviations, is within the process tolerance limits) is a useful measure of how well the process is likely to produce output consistently within tolerance.

■ To give an early indication of a process drifting out of control, control limits are drawn within the tolerance limits.

5 Applying the techniques

The techniques you have learned in this session of the workbook are used in **statistical process control (SPC)**.

5.1 Statistical process control

Statistical process control is the general term applied to the use of statistics to analyse data from processes (or process outputs) as an aid to solving quality problems.

We used SPC in the last section, when we determined control limits for a machining process.

The most common application of SPC is in manufacturing processes, but it has also been successfully applied to such diverse problems as keeping telephone costs within acceptable limits, and cutting down accident rates. In fact, SPC can usually be applied where:

■ there are many individual events taking place, and
■ it is desired to set and maintain control limits.

Some possible applications of SPC are as follows:

> A parcel delivery service company gives a guarantee to its customers on delivery times: 'If we're late with your parcel, you get double your money back!' The company knows that a lot of organization goes into getting a parcel from source to destination. It needs to be sure that its work processes are capable, and that any drifting towards an 'out of limits' situation is detected well before it happens.

> A supermarket selling perishable goods works to a system of 'best before' and 'display until/use by' dates. If goods stay on the shelves too long, they will be wasted. A method of quality control using SPC aims to keep the amount of waste below a certain level. Records of the

numbers of out-of-date items for each product line are kept. Used together with sales figures, these give store managers an early indication of changes in customer preferences, as well as helping to keep waste and costs down.

A bank uses operators to key in vast amounts of data. A certain level of error rate is inevitable, but the aim always has to be to keep the number of keying errors to a minimum. Certain types of critical data are always double-checked, and the rest is sampled. Running records are kept of each operator's performance.

A garden plant supplier sells large numbers of plants to garden centres and DIY stores. Quality criteria for each type of plant are defined, including height, number of flowers, number of leaves, and so on. Each batch is sampled, to check that the defined criteria are being met. SPC helps to give an early indication of any fall in quality.

Of course, SPC is simply a tool to help people make the right decisions. SPC won't tell you **what** to do to improve performance. But it will indicate **whether** you need to take action, and **whether** or not those actions have had the desired effects.

SPC is used in answering the following questions about a process:

- Is the process operating in a stable and predictable way?
- By how much can we expect the process to vary?
- Knowing the answers to these questions, what targets or control limits could be set?

Suppose a work operation is varying, so that some of the results are outside acceptable limits.

- The first thing you would want to know is **how much** variation there is in the process before anything is changed.

  Here is where statistical analysis of the process data will help.

- Then you would need to decide on the appropriate action: perhaps changing a setting, replacing a machine, or giving staff more training.

  Statistics won't tell you what to do – only that some action needs to be taken. Here is where your experience and knowledge of the process come into play in devising an appropriate action.

■ Once you have taken this action, you want to know how successful it has been.

Here again, statistics should be of great help.

Let's look at the steps typically used in statistical process control. The relevance of the techniques you have learned in this workbook will then become more obvious.

Step	Activity	Comment	Techniques typically used
1	Data from the process in question are collected and displayed.	The data must be accurate and should reflect the process performance. Decisions which have to be taken include what size of sample to collect, and how frequently to take samples.	**Sampling** **Graphs**
2	This data are plotted on a control chart.	This is what we learned to do in the last section. The range, as well as the mean, may be plotted.	**Range** **Mean** **Control charts**
3	Once the process has settled down, its process capability is determined.	If you recall, capability is the ability of a work process to produce output within a desired tolerance for a sustained period.	**Process capability**
4	Control limits are calculated.	There may be pre-defined specification limits, as in our examples. In other processes, there may be no imposed limits: the aim is then to control the process to limits that are as tight as possible.	**Control limits**

5.2 Using statistics to help solve problems

There are many applications for the quality techniques we have looked at in this workbook. When approaching problems involving these techniques, you may find the following hints useful:

- Make sure the data you collect reflects the performance of the process.
- Use charts and diagrams to display the data, so that it can be understood more easily.
- Be patient and careful – don't jump to conclusions.
- Use statistics to help you determine whether the standard you want to achieve is really achievable.
- Use statistics to help analyze results.
- Make only one change at a time – and then use statistics to tell you what difference the change has made to your problem.
- Keep on learning more about statistics, so that you have lots of statistical tools which you can use at will.

Self-assessment 4 · 20 mins

1 A team member is sampling boxes of compact discs. Each box contains twenty discs. A particular box contains the following faulty discs: one scratched disc, two over-size discs and three discs with incorrect labels. The team member picks out one disc at random.

a What is the probability of selecting a disc with an incorrect label?
b What is the probability of selecting a disc with a fault of any kind?

The box then passes to a second team member who picks out another disc (the first disc was replaced, whether or not it was faulty).

c What is the probability of either person finding a faulty disc?
d How can the team change the system so that they become certain to find all the faults?

2 A DIY chain receives wall tiles in cases each containing 440 tiles and samples cases for defects. They work to an AQL of 0.4 per cent.

How many samples should be taken from each box? What is the maximum number of defects that should be allowed in the sample for the box to be accepted? What is the minimum number of defects that should result in the box being rejected?

Use the following sampling inspection tables in your calculation.

| Batch size code letter | Sample size | Acceptance quality limit, AQL, in percent non-conforming items and noncomformities per 100 items (normal inspection) ||||||||||||

Batch size code letter	Sample size	0.040 Ac Re	0.065 Ac Re	0.10 Ac Re	0.15 Ac Re	0.25 Ac Re	0.4 Ac Re	0.65 Ac Re	1.0 Ac Re	1.5 Ac Re	2.5 Ac Re	4 Ac Re	6.5 Ac Re
F	20	↓	↓	↓	↓	↓	↓	0 1	↑	↓	1 2	2 3	3 4
G	32	↓	↓	↓	↓	↓	0 1	↑	↓	1 2	2 3	3 4	5 6
H	50	↓	↓	↓	↓	0 1	↑	↓	1 2	2 3	3 4	5 6	7 8
J	80	↓	↓	↓	0 1	↑	↓	1 2	2 3	3 4	5 6	7 8	10 11
K	125	↓	↓	0 1	↑	↓	1 2	2 3	3 4	5 6	7 8	10 11	14 15
L	200	↓	0 1	↑	↓	1 2	2 3	3 4	5 6	7 8	10 11	14 15	21 22
M	315	0 1	↑	↓	1 2	2 3	3 4	5 6	7 8	10 11	14 15	21 22	↑
N	500	↑	↓	1 2	2 3	3 4	5 6	7 8	10 11	14 15	21 22	↑	↑

Lot size	
From	**To**
281	500
501	1200
1201	3200
3201	10000
10001	35000
35001	150000
15001	500000
500001	and over

General inspection levels		
I	II	III
F	H	J
G	J	K
H	K	L
J	L	M
K	M	N
L	N	P
M	P	Q
N	Q	R

3   A pizza restaurant aims to deliver an order, within a five-mile radius, in under fifteen minutes. A sample of five measurements are taken each day of the length of time taken for a delivery, and the following results are found for a ten-day period:

Sample means of delivery time in minutes (the mean of each sample of five daily timings)				
13.6	12.4	11.8	14.2	13.2
12.8	11.6	14.8	12.6	13.0

a   Work out the mean of sample means and the standard deviation.
b   Sketch a suitable graph of these values, showing control limits. (Hint: there is no 'lower tolerance limit', and the values are all above 10, so the vertical scale could be marked from 10 to 15.)
c   Decide whether this work process is capable.

Answers to these questions can be found on pages 116–17.

6 Summary

■ The idea of **sampling** is that only some items are checked. Provided certain defined rules are followed, the proportion of defects in the sample should give an indication of the proportion of defects in the whole quantity. The more samples that are taken, the greater the chances of finding defects.

■ **Acceptable quality level (AQL)** is the maximum percentage of defects in a sample that can be considered acceptable as a process average. It does **not** mean that it is acceptable to make mistakes.

■ A problem frequently encountered in quality control is the monitoring of work processes to make sure that results are **within tolerance**, and to detect when they are **drifting out of tolerance**.

■ Sampling is used, and the sample means are plotted on a control chart. The **tolerance limits** are drawn on the chart.

■ **Process capability** – the ability of a work process to produce output within a desired tolerance for a sustained period – can be determined by calculating the mean of its sample means, plus and minus three standard deviations, and finding whether this is within the process tolerance limits.

■ To give an early indication of a process drifting out of control, **control limits** are drawn within the tolerance limits.

■ **Statistical process control (SPC)** is the general term applied to the use of statistics to analyse data from processes or process outputs, as an aid in solving quality problems.

Performance checks

1 Quick quiz

Jot down the answers to the following questions on *Achieving Quality.*

Question 1   Complete the sentence: 'The starting point for quality is . . . .'

_____

Question 2   What's the difference between a **producer** and a **supplier**?

_____

_____

Question 3   What's the difference between **design quality** and the **quality of conformance**?

_____

_____

_____

_____

Question 4   Which people in the organization are involved in quality?

_____

Question 5   Briefly, how can a manager help to 'set a culture for quality'?

_____

_____

_____

Question 6   Briefly, what is meant by 'continuous improvement'?

_____

_____

_____

Question 7   Given the choice between two organizations offering identical products, what greater assurances do you have by buying from the supplier with ISO 9000 accreditation?

_____

_____

_____

Question 8   What is contained in a quality manual?

_____

_____

Question 9   Why is it important that raw materials, services and other 'bought-in' goods be traceable to the company that supplies the product?

_____

_____

_____

_____

Question 10   Under ISO 9000, is sampling of products for conformity allowed?

_____

Question 11   'If we take any large population of things or people, and measure some characteristic, the distribution of the data will be normal.' Briefly explain what this sentence means.

_____

_____

_____

_____

Question 12   Explain the meaning of the term 'acceptable quality level (AQL)'.

_____

_____

_____

Question 13   What is meant by the term 'process capability'?

_____

_____

_____

Question 14   What's the difference between a **tolerance limit** and a **control limit**?

_____

_____

_____

_____

Answers to these questions can be found on pages 119–20.

2 Workbook assessment

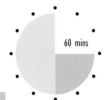

60 mins

Read the following case incident and then deal with the instruction that follows, writing your answers on a separate sheet of paper.

Harfleet Plastics is a small company in the business of manufacturing goods for domestic equipment. Its Managing Director, Alan Pursloe, would like the company to receive ISO 9000 accreditation, and calls you in as a consultant.

After a preliminary investigation you discover the following facts:

a In order to 'stay competitive', the company buys raw materials at the cheapest price, regardless of who the supplier is.

b Although most customers are satisfied with Harfleet's quality, there have been a few complaints, which the company has responded to in a number of ways. As Alan Pursloe says, 'You have to be careful – some people complain about any little thing. We're delivering products that have to be made quickly and cheaply. We try not to cut corners, but people get what they pay for. There's no time to inspect everything and sometimes a machine will drift out of tolerance, which you can't do much about until it happens.'

c   There are two points of inspection: materials are sampled when they are received, and the final product is sampled before shipment.

d   The company has a small group of design engineers and they sometimes get another company to design items for them. Alternatively, the customer will specify a design. However, drawings and specifications are not always evident in the production department; the reason for this is that 'people generally know what they're doing – they can ask the engineers if they're in any doubt'.

e   Some of the test equipment seems to be old and of dubious reliability.

f   The Production Manager, Sertan Lescott, also doubles as the Quality Assurance Manager. When you attend a management meeting you observe a discussion about marketing, during which the Marketing Manager, Lesley Ackerman, is heard to remark: 'Don't bring me into discussions about quality – I've enough to worry about. You stick to your job and I'll stick to mine.'

g   When you ask about training, you are told: 'Many jobs are unskilled. People doing these don't need much training and they largely learn on the job. Of course, more skilled people have their own qualifications and training, mostly gained before they joined us. But we don't concern ourselves too much about certificates, provided the job gets done efficiently.'

Write a report to the Managing Director, describing your recommendations. What should your report contain? Make out a list of specific points that you can use to develop for a more detailed report. (Try to include points based on what you have learned from all four sessions of this workbook.) You do not need to write more than a page or so.

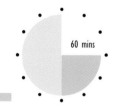

3 Work-based assignment

S/NVQs
AI.1, AI.3

The time guide for this assignment gives you an approximate idea of how long it is likely to take you to write up your findings. You will find you need to spend some additional time gathering information, perhaps talking to colleagues, and thinking about the assignment. The result of your efforts should be presented on separate sheets of paper.

Your written response to this assignment may provide the basis of appropriate evidence for your S/NVQ portfolio.

The assignment is designed to help you to demonstrate your personal competence in:

- building teams;
- communicating;
- focusing on results;
- thinking and taking decisions.

What you have to do

Choose **either** A (for S/NVQ A1.1) **or** B (for S/NVQ A1.3) below.

A Having learned something of statistical process control, you may feel that it can be usefully applied to work processes carried out by your team. If so, investigate the matter further, preferably after discussing it with someone who is experienced in using these techniques, such as the Quality Assurance Manager.

Having agreed what you are going to do and how you are going to do it, with your manager and the people involved, follow the approach you have learned about in *Achieving Quality*. Your objective is to develop and operate a statistical process control system that enables you to ensure that the process you manage is operating within acceptable quality limits. Records of your sampling plan, data collection, control charts and any reports you produce on quality as a result can all be used in your portfolio.

B Select at least one of the following areas of quality management and draw up a brief report showing where quality problems arise, identifying the causes of these problems and possible ways of overcoming them, and making recommendations for improvement.

- contract review;
- design control;
- document or data control;
- purchasing;
- product identification or traceability;
- process control;
- inspection and testing;
- inspection;
- test or measuring equipment;
- control of non-conforming product;
- corrective and preventative action;
- storage or packaging;
- training.

Reflect and review

1 Reflect and review

Now that you have completed your work on *Achieving Quality*, let us review our workbook objectives.

■ When you have completed this workbook you will be better able to explain the meaning and purpose of quality.

We began by discussing what quality is and what it isn't. The organization's starting point for quality is always the needs of its customers, and quality can be summarized as 'fitness for purpose'. Quality does not mean offering gold-plated luxury goods or sophisticated services to people who have no need for them.

Therefore, producers and suppliers must:

■ know what their customers need and want;
■ find ways of designing products to meet those needs and wants;
■ define quality standards;
■ ensure that these standards are adhered to.

■ Are you convinced that your team has a good understanding of quality's meaning and purpose? _____

■ If not, what training or instruction would be useful to them, in this respect?

_____

_____

_____

_____

Our next objective was:

- When you have completed this workbook you will be better able to describe some sound approaches to quality management.

As we have discussed, effective quality management includes:

- displaying commitment;
- setting standards;
- providing resources;
- allowing employees to take responsibility for standards;
- setting a culture for quality.

All this is very easy to say, but requires a great deal of planning and effort to put it into practice.

- How might you display more commitment to quality? Write down one thing you could do.

_____

_____

- What further resource might you provide which would make it easier for your team to realize their quality goals?

_____

_____

The third objective was:

- When you have completed this workbook you will be better able to summarize the contents and purpose of ISO 9000:2000.

Session B contained a broad summary of the contents and purpose of this standard, so we won't list them all again. As you will have noticed, ISO 9000 imposes a good many demands on organizations and, as you might expect, accreditation to the standard is not easily achieved.

- If you need to find out more about ISO 9000, how will you set about doing so?

_____

_____

_____

- How could you make your team better informed about this standard?

_____

_____

_____

The next objective was:

■ When you have completed this workbook you will be better able to carry out simple statistical calculations related to quality control.

In statistics, we have looked at the mean, the range and the standard deviation. If you are not mathematically inclined you may have struggled with this section. If so, you can decide whether you can afford to forget all about it or struggle on and try to learn more. The book listed under Extension 3 may be worth looking at, or you could perhaps find a convenient evening class.

■ What further action will you take to develop your skills in statistics?

_____

_____

_____

The final objective was:

■ When you have completed this workbook you will be better able to recognize how the techniques of statistical process control can be usefully applied to work processes.

We have seen that SPC is not confined to manufacturing industry. All kinds of producers and suppliers can benefit from these techniques.

■ How could you benefit from SPC?

_____

_____

_____

■ What could you do to learn more about the subject?

_____

_____

_____

2 Action plan

Use this plan to further develop for yourself a course of action you want to take. Make a note in the left-hand column of the issues or problems you want to tackle, and then decide what you intend to do, and make a note in column 2.

The resources you need might include time, materials, information or money. You may need to negotiate for some of them, but they could be something easily acquired, like half an hour of somebody's time, or a chapter of a book. Put whatever you need in column 3. No plan means anything without a timescale, so put a realistic target completion date in column 4.

Finally, describe the outcome you want to achieve as a result of this plan, whether it is for your own benefit or advancement, or a more efficient way of doing things.

Desired outcomes			
1 Issues	2 Action	3 Resources	4 Target completion
Actual outcomes			

3 Extensions

Extension 1

Book   *Business Process Improvement*
Author   H James Harrington
Publisher   McGraw-Hill Education, first edition 1991

This is a very practical book on how to put the ideas of quality improvement into practice, in a straightforward and structured way.

Extension 2

Book   *ISO 9000 Quality Systems Handbook*
Author   David Hoyle
Publisher   Butterworth-Heinemann, first edition 2001

This is a comprehensive and practical guide, covering over 250 requirements of the new ISO 9000:2000 standard. It includes useful checklists, flowcharts, related standards and bibliography. It is ideal if you are working in an orgranization intending to be accredited to the new standard.

Extension 3

Book   *Statistics*
Author   Frank Owen and Ron Jones
Publisher   Pearson Education, fourth edition (1994)

You may find this useful as a general introduction to statistics, including the quality control aspects. However, there are plenty of other books on the same subject.

Extension 4

Book   *A Practical Approach to Quality Control*
Author   R.H. Caplen
Publisher   Random House Business Books, first edition (1996)

This book deals with the technical aspects of quality, covering the City & Guilds syllabus on the subject.

These extensions can be taken up via your ILM Centre. They will either have them or will arrange that you have access to them. However, it may be more convenient to check out the materials with your personnel or training people at work – they may well give you access. There are other good reasons for approaching your own people; for example, they will become aware of your interest and you can involve them in your development.

4 Answers to self-assessment questions

Self-assessment 1 on page 13

1 a Quality is another word for 'superior'.

Quality is not another word for 'superior'. On the contrary, quality means producing and supplying products that are fit for their purpose, and meet the customer's needs.

b The organization's quality experts have the main responsibility for quality.

Everyone in an organization shares the responsibility for quality.

c The marketing and design of a product is quite separate from its quality aspects.

All aspects of a product affect its quality, including marketing and design.

d Quality is everyone's business, so managers have no special role to play.

Quality **is** everyone's business, but managers have an important responsibility to lead the way in quality, as in other things.

2 a Fitness for purpose.   iii Quality

b The totality of features and characteristics   iii Quality
of a product or service that bear on its
ability to satisfy stated or implied needs.

c The degree to which the specification of the   v Design quality
product satisfies customers' wants and
expectations.

d The degree to which the product conforms   iv Conformance
to specifications, when it is transferred to   quality
the customer.   or
                                                                              i Process quality

e The operational techniques and activities   ii Quality control
that are used to fulfil requirements for
quality.

Reflect and review

1 Product standards set out requirements for particular types of product; systems standards set out requirements for the good organization and management of processes.

2 Services, software, hardware and processed materials.

3 Reasons for adopting ISO 9000 include the following.

- Because the organization feels the need to control or improve the quality of its products.
- To reduce costs, or become more competitive.
- Because customers expect them to do so.
- Because the organization wants to supply products to a government body that refuses to do business with organizations unless their quality management systems are independently verified.

4 In brief, control of documents means controlling versions, ensuring documents are approved, and preventing the use of obsolete documents.

5 A quality policy should make a specific commitment to continuous improvement.

6 SMART = Specific, Measurable, Achievable, Relevant, Time bound.

7 An organization's human resources should have the right experience, education, training and skills to do the job that they do.

8 All or any part of Section 7 of ISO 9001 be ignored if the organization cannot apply it because of the nature of the organization or the nature of the product.

9 Requirements related to an organization's products are determined mainly by the customer. However, it may also be necessary to adhere to external regulations and organizational requirements, such as marketing and cost control.

10 The organization should appoint a specific person or group of people who will review and approve each stage of the design, and sign it off so it passes on to the next stage. Likewise all changes should be subject to approval.

11 Examples of controls over production and service provision include the following.

- Information that describes the product should be available.
- Work instructions should set out how the product is made.
- Any equipment used should be suitable for the job.
- Monitoring and measuring devices should be available and properly used.

12 A 'special' process is any process where it is impractical or unsafe to perform tests and inspections during the actual process. Usually the quality of the work can only be fully validated by destructive testing or prolonged use of the product.

13 Section 8 of ISO 9001 is about 'remedial processes'. The requirements are intended to ensure that the organization makes the effort to find out whether it is conforming to its quality objectives and takes appropriate action if not.

14 An internal audit is an investigation carried out by an organization's staff (as opposed to an independent external auditor) to determine whether a system's processes, checks and controls are working properly and the system is doing what it is supposed to do.

15 An organization controls nonconforming products by taking measures to prevent the delivery of nonconforming products and by eliminating or correcting product nonconformities.

Self-assessment 3 on pages 70–2

1

$$\text{Total} = 900, \text{ so mean} = \frac{\text{total}}{\text{number of value}} = \frac{900}{20} = 45$$

$$\text{Range} = 98 - 7 = 91$$

2

Step	Calculation
	Data: the typing speed of five typists in words per minute: 80, 57, 72, 48, 63
1 Work out the mean of the set of values.	Total 320. Mean = $\frac{320}{5}$ = 64 wpm
2 Subtract the mean from each value, to give the 'differences'.	80 − 64 = 16 57 − 64 = −7 72 − 64 = 8 48 − 64 = −16 63 − 64 = −1
3 Take each of these differences and square it: multiply it by itself.	16 × 16 = 256 −7 × −7 = 49 8 × 8 = 64 −16 × −16 = 256 −1 × −1 = 1
4 Add up these squares.	256 + 49 + 64 + 256 + 1 = 626
5 Divide this sum by the number of items. The result is called the 'variance'.	$\frac{626}{5}$ = 125.2
6 Take the square root of the variance; this gives the standard deviation.	$\sigma = \sqrt{125.2}$ = 11.19 wpm (approx.)

3   Compare your sketch with the one shown below:

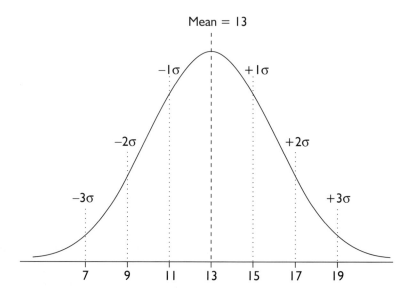

4   The answers are:

   a   C and E
   b   C and F, or B and E
   c   C and G, or A and E.

**Self-assessment 4
on pages 97–8**

1   a   There are three discs with incorrect labels, so the probability of finding one
        of these is $\frac{3}{20}$ = 0.15.
    b   There are six faulty discs, so the probability of finding one of them is
        $\frac{6}{20}$ = 0.3.
    c   To work out the probability of one action or another, we add the
        probabilities: 0.3 + 0.3 = 0.6.
    d   Strictly speaking, there is no way to be sure of finding all the faults.
        However, 100 per cent inspection will increase the chances considerably.

2   Since you have no reason not to you should use column II to find out the
    appropriate letter. For a batch of 440 you should use letter H.

    Row H with an AQL of 0.4 per cent gives an upwards arrow pointing to row
    G.

    Row G shows us that the size of the sample that should be taken from each
    box is 32. If **any** defects are found in the sample the batch should be rejected.
    Otherwise, it should be accepted.

3   a   The total of the values = 130. The mean of sample means = $\frac{130}{10}$ = 13. The
        standard deviation = 0.951.

b A suitable graph is shown below:

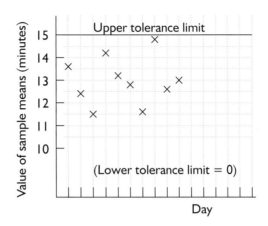

c We don't have a lower tolerance limit, so we can't simply apply the formula. The question is: 'Is the mean plus three standard deviations less than the upper tolerance limit?'

Mean + 3σ = 13 + (3 $\times$ 0.951) = 15.853. But the upper tolerance limit is fifteen minutes, so this work process is not capable. (Somehow, the service must be speeded up, or we can expect late deliveries – sooner or later!)

5 Answers to activities

Activity 3 on page 6

The answer is 'All of the above': everyone in the company must take responsibility for quality. Quality is not something that can be added on at the end of the line.

Activity 25 on page 66

As you will see from the next diagram, the normal curve moves along the axis as the mean changes.

This is what three sets of data with the same 'spread', but with different means, looks like.

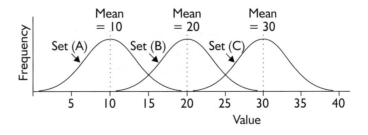

Activity 37
on pages 89–90

a The total of the values = 70, so the mean of sample means = 7. The standard deviation = 3.435.

A suitable graph is shown below:

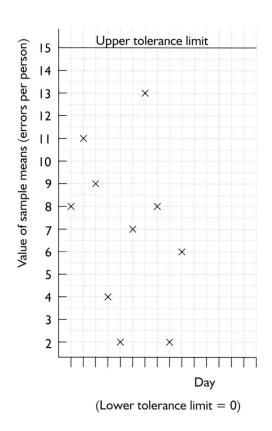

(Lower tolerance limit = 0)

b We don't have a lower tolerance limit, so we can't simply apply the formula. The question is: 'Is the mean plus three standard deviations less than the upper tolerance limit?'

Mean + 3σ = 7 + (3 × 3.435) = 17.305. But the upper tolerance limit is ten errors per person, so this work process is not capable of meeting the management target.

6 Answers to the quick quiz

Answer 1   The starting point for quality is in the needs of the customer.

Answer 2   A **producer** generates goods or services for sale. A **supplier** offers goods or services for sale.

Answer 3   **Design quality** is the degree to which the specification of the product satisfies customers' wants and expectations. The **quality of conformance** is the degree to which the product conforms to specifications, when it is transferred to the customer.

Answer 4   Everybody!

Answer 5   A manager needs to behave as if he or she cares about quality, and has a commitment to it, so encouraging the rest of the staff to follow suit.

Answer 6   Continuous improvement means carrying out many detailed improvements to products, procedures and practices, over a long period.

Answer 7   The organization with ISO 9000 accreditation has proved that its quality system is under control, so that it is able to ensure delivery of products meeting customers' requirements.

Answer 8   A quality manual contains all the procedures for implementing the quality system.

Answer 9   An organization wishing to deliver quality products must have control over its suppliers. Should bought-in goods and services be faulty, the supplier must be traced so that corrective action can be taken, and to ensure that the problem does not recur.

Answer 10   Yes: 100 per cent inspection is not required.

Answer 11   The graph of a normal distribution shows a characteristic bell-shaped curve, symmetrical about its mean, and whose width depends on the standard deviation of the data. All large populations will tend to have graphs of this type.

Answer 12   Acceptable quality level (AQL) is the maximum percentage of defectives in a sample, that can be considered acceptable as a process average.

Answer 13   Process capability is the ability of a work process to produce output within a desired tolerance for a sustained period.

Answer 14   A **tolerance limit** is the outer boundary of tolerable values for a process. **Control limits** are set within tolerance limits to give an early indication that a process may be drifting out of tolerance.

7 Certificate

Completion of this certificate by an authorized person shows that you have worked through all the parts of this workbook and satisfactorily completed the assessments. The certificate provides a record of what you have done that may be used for exemptions or as evidence of prior learning against other nationally certificated qualifications.

Pergamon Flexible Learning and ILM are always keen to refine and improve their products. One of the key sources of information to help this process are people who have just used the product. If you have any information or views, good or bad, please pass these on.

INSTITUTE OF LEADERSHIP & MANAGEMENT

SUPERSERIES

Achieving Quality

....

has satisfactorily completed this workbook

Name of signatory   ....

Position   ....

Signature   ....

Date   ....

Official stamp

Fourth Edition